MW00861512

Patchwork
Sassaman
Style Recipes for Dazzling Quilts!

Jane Sassaman

Editor in Chief: **Linda Chang Teufel**

Graphic Design and Illustration: **Kimberly Koloski**

Photography: **Gregory Gantner**

Copy Editor: **Pat Radloff**

Library of Congress Cataloging-in-Publication Data

Library of Congress Control Number: 2012934651

Sassaman, Jane
Patchwork Sassaman Style / Jane Sassaman

p.cm.

1. Patchwork
2. Quilting
I. Title

ISBN# 978-0-9818860-3-9

Dragon Threads Ltd.
Extraordinary Textile Arts Books

490 Tucker Drive
Worthington, OH 43085

www.DragonThreads.com

This book is dedicated to all my fabric
fondling friends who have encouraged,
inspired, humored and stitched with
me on this colorful quilting journey.

Jane Sassaman

Introduction 7

History and Designing Fabric 8

Principles of Using
Personality Prints 14

Sewing Basics: Equipment 16

Patchwork Basics 20

Three Kinds of Cuts 27

Design Aids 30

About The Recipes 33

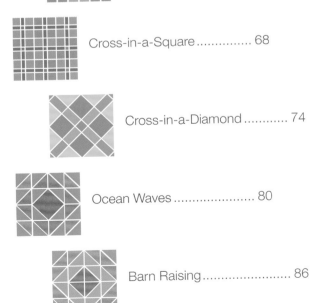

Whole Cloth 34

Amish Bars 38

One + Four Patch 44

Checkerboard Plaid 50

Radiating Diamonds 56

Fancy Nine-Patch 62

Cross-in-a-Square 68

Cross-in-a-Diamond 74

Ocean Waves 80

Barn Raising 86

Mirrored Triangles 92

Cross-in-a-Cross 100

Quilting and Finishing............ 160

Thousand Mountains 108

Wrap Up.............................. 165

LeMoyne Star 114

Acknowledgements 166

Broken Star 122

Grandmother's Flower Garden.... 128

The Fan 134

Big-Hearted Quilt............... 140

Butterfly Quilt 146

Flower Pots 152

This book has been written for all of the quilters who love fancy fabrics but don't quite know how to use them and for the new "modern" quilters who have already embraced personality prints and made them part of their creative palette. So the goal of this book is to show some basic ideas for using those big, bold and beautiful fabrics.

These quilt designs are inspired by simple traditional quilt patterns. Consequently, there is plenty of room for flexibility. So much of the creative decision-making happens during the process of making the quilt. This process is part of the fun. The surprising relationships between fabrics can guide a quilt as you work.

Quilting is an organic process which includes listening and looking for the character in the cloth…color, line, pattern, scale and then mixing characters to make an interesting reaction. Just like in the kitchen, we can personalize the recipe according to the ingredients at hand or to suit our own taste and make it spicier, sweeter, juicier or richer. A personality print can add some unexpected and exciting flavors to these simple recipes.

So these ideas are just a place to begin. You will see variations within each category and I will attempt to describe the creative decision-making along the way.

My affair with fabric began early. As a child, I was delighted to discover exotic fabrics beyond the practical calicos and kettle cloth of everyday clothing. Later, the British Invasion's lavish use of rich velvets, brocades and lace acted as a counterpoint to the space age vinyl and mylar. Color during this period was wild, too. Betsey Johnson pink, Beatles psychedelic and Peter Max posters ruled the day.

All of this was happening when I was an art student and came under the influence of William Morris and the Arts and Crafts Movement.

These 19th-century artists lived in a similar period of unrest and creativity during the Industrial Revolution in England.

"Have nothing in your houses which you do not know to be useful or believe to be beautiful," was Morris's golden rule. His followers were encouraged to use nature as their primary source of inspiration and to take joy in handwork, which was believed to be an antidote to mechanization. Consequently, there was a revived interest in the decorative arts. Morris, himself, designed a wide range of objects, including embroidery, tapestry, textiles, wallpaper, books and type fonts. The Arts and Crafts philosophy spread throughout Europe, North America and Japan and influenced many of my favorite late 19th-century artists, each of whom designed fabric, among other things.

My own passion for the decorative arts and handwork have been the seeds from which my career as a quilter and fabric designer has grown. I began quilting in 1980. My art quilts are primarily appliquéd compositions of stylized shapes from nature. As the work evolved, many of my compositions began to have an "implied pattern" or rhythm and repetition of elements that suggested the regular repeat of a printed textile design. Creating a quilt is a very satisfying process, but it is also so labor intensive that I

Consequently, my yearly schedule is built around the fabric designing season, which is roughly from December to March, the deep winter months here in the Midwest. It takes a lot of doodling, concentration and drawing to bring a coherent series of designs together. A theme is the first thing to be determined. But sometimes the theme can change in mid-stream; it's an organic process just like designing a quilt. But no matter the thread of the theme, most designs are autobiographical and portray favorite plants and insects in my home environment or those that I have admired during my travels.

could only produce a few quilts every year, depending on their size. For a designer with lots of ideas, this limited output of quilts/images was frustrating.

In 2002 I was invited to design fabric for an exciting new company called Free Spirit, and I jumped at the opportunity. Here was the chance I'd been waiting for; a chance to contribute to the "design of my time."

For the first line, *Jane's Exotic Garden*, nature, as always, was my mentor but I was also guided by the historic fabrics that I admired so much from Morris to Marimekko. I wanted my patterns as well, to be large scale, graphic and colorful…similar to my art quilts, too. Essentially, these designs could mirror my appliqué style, but with the extra detail which printing could enable. In other words, I strived to design "art by the yard."

I had a great time putting the collection together, nine designs in three different colorways. It was a thrilling day when the first "strike-offs" arrived with my name printed on the selvedge! Since then I have continued to produce a yearly collection.

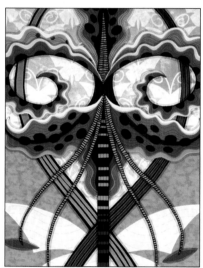

Over the years I have accumulated motifs that "speak my language" and they have become part of my artistic ammunition.

There is often a direct connection between my appliqué and my fabric designs. They are constantly cross-fertilizing and building off each other. They share many common characters and shapes. Over the years I have accumulated motifs that "speak my language" and they have become part of my artistic ammunition. For example, dandelions are a favorite symbol that has been featured in both mediums. To me the dandelion represents a tenacious life force; an overwhelming naive stubbornness. It is totally unaware of its reputation.

Spirals are another shape that I love and utilize in all my designs. Spirals illustrate the movement of growth and add energy to a composition.

I have also used butterflies in both my appliqué and my fabric design. They are a magical and ethereal metaphor for beauty and can add playfulness or mystery, depending on the butterfly.

But usually my fabrics portray some of the colorful favorites that we grow in our garden every year... zinnias, iris, bleeding heart plus a few dragonflies, spiders, birds and butterflies. The irony is that I am designing in the gray days of winter! Perhaps that's why the fabrics turn out so bright. Each collection has its own story to tell.

I begin each inkling of an idea with a pencil drawing and then work it into a basic repeat, which is determined by the screen sizes at the factory. Depending on the scale, I usually use a large architectural printer to scale the design up or down and then print multiples to cut up and lay out in a nearly perfect scaled repeat pattern. After the scale and repeat are set, I begin to fill in the details by hand.

When most of the details are determined, I will redraw the design as nicely as possible with permanent black ink on velum or tracing paper. Then it is scanned into the computer and I begin the tedious, but enjoyable, job of cleaning up the drawing in Photoshop with the help of my precious Wacom tablet and stylus. The master drawing is saved before the color play begins.

I begin by perfecting each design in a single colorway, which becomes the master template for the other two colorways. Designing colorways is equivalent to designing a silk screen. Let's say your design has

three colors, so you have three screens, one for each color. For each colorway you must use the same three screens, but print them with different colors. You can't add or subtract screens, so the color changes must be thought out carefully and look natural. I make tons of test prints along the way…my Epson ink and paper bills are quite remarkable.

In the designing "zone," all thoughts revolve around the design possibilities. Awake or asleep the gears are grinding. Exercise has also become an important part of the process for a clearer head and happier body. I relish every minute of my winters in the studio.

When all the colors have been determined I print the final art and pin it to my work wall in color groups to make sure all the designs are working together. Then I make another set of prints with numbers that correspond to large color swatches for the factory to match.

After three to four months of concentration, it is an emotional day when I ship my "babies" off to Free Spirit/Westminster where they nurse and supervise the designs onto fabric and guide it to your favorite store.

When the fabric is printed, it is a totally independent creation and has its own dynamics. As a designer I love the challenge of transforming the fabrics into their next incarnation as quilts and other accessories. It is the next sequence in the creative process, but now the fabric is my guide. In this book, it is my pleasure to show you some of the quilts that have evolved by "listening to the fabric."

When the fabric is printed, it is a totally independent creation and has its own dynamics.

Early Birds by Jane Sassaman

tminster Fibers # PWJS36 Cheeky Checks 1 2

Early Birds by Jane Sassaman for *FreeSpirit*   Westminster Fibers # PWJS41 Prairie Poppy

Early Birds by Jane Sassaman for *FreeSpirit*   Westminster Fibers # F

The art of patchwork has a rich history and tradition, which is much revered by the modern quilter. But today's quilters and crafters are also influenced by the living world around them. They are computer savvy and interested in contemporary trends in design and fashion.

The vibrancy of the crafting community has spurred creativity throughout the "do-it-yourself" industry. One of the most refreshing results of this prolific production has been the wealth of new fabric designed for contemporary crafting. Makers have never had such an abundance or variety of textile designs to choose from.

The new textiles are designed as "art" for use. They are infused with "attitude", energy and personality. That is why I call them *personality prints*.

Personality prints

A personality print is designed to be the star of the show. They are passionate and speak for themselves. They are delicious straight off the bolt. In fact, they are designed to be appreciated in their unadulterated, uncut state.

But they can be hard-working players when used as part of an ensemble in a quilt. Personality prints can shoulder most of the heavy work if used respectfully. This means you need to listen and learn from your fabric before you begin. In fact, all printed fabrics have characteristics to take into consideration before using them in your quilt.

I have been listening to my big, bold and beautiful fabrics for over ten years and I have learned some basic principles for using personality prints for patchwork.

1. Keep it simple!

Personality Prints are so robust it is best to use them in very large and simple compositions. This is why traditional pieced patchwork patterns work wonderfully with big prints. The simple geometry of patchwork gives just enough formality to discipline a wild print.

2. The bigger the print, the bigger the block.

The block is the basic building unit in patchwork. You can make a quilt pattern in any scale. A 6" block can just as easily be 12" or 18". And the scale of your print should dictate the initial size of your block. "Super size" your traditional quilt pattern for super-sized prints.

3. Use simple fabrics as supporting players.

Solid colored fabrics, tone-on-tone and simple prints can bring out the best in a personality print. Simple prints can supply focus and breathing room in an exuberant quilt.

4. Contrast creates drama.

Too much of the same thing is boring, even big prints. Mixing contrasting colors, shapes, textures and scale can make a composition more interesting and dramatic…light and dark, quiet and busy, round and pointy, plain and fancy, large and small.

5. What you don't see is often as important as what you do see.

In other words, cropping has a huge effect in a patchwork composition. The edge of each shape reacts to its neighbor. This reaction can create a sharp line or a soft blend, depending on where the design was cut. Losing part of a motif by cropping can often strengthen your overall design.

6. Symmetrical fabrics yearn to be fussy cut.

Patchwork is based on geometry. Symmetrical designs inside symmetrical shapes are natural partners. This unbeatable combination can make incredible kaleidoscopic effects.

7. One good butterfly deserves another.

Many fabric designs are pictorial. They have been designed around a theme…birds, daisies, teacups, trees, etc. You can have great fun by designing a quilt around a favorite printed motif or subject.

8. Be flexible…quilts can improve along the way.

Allow yourself to change the original concept of your design as you work. Don't get stuck in a preconceived idea. Sometimes unplanned design decisions can make a better quilt.

9. One print can be used in several colors.

Using the same print in several color ways can create some radically sophisticated patchwork with very little work on your part.

10. The back of your quilt can be just as awesome as the front!

A quilt has two sides to make an impact, so don't neglect the back.

11. Let the fabric do the work!

Let your personality prints shine! After all, that's what they were designed to do.

Let the fabric do the work!

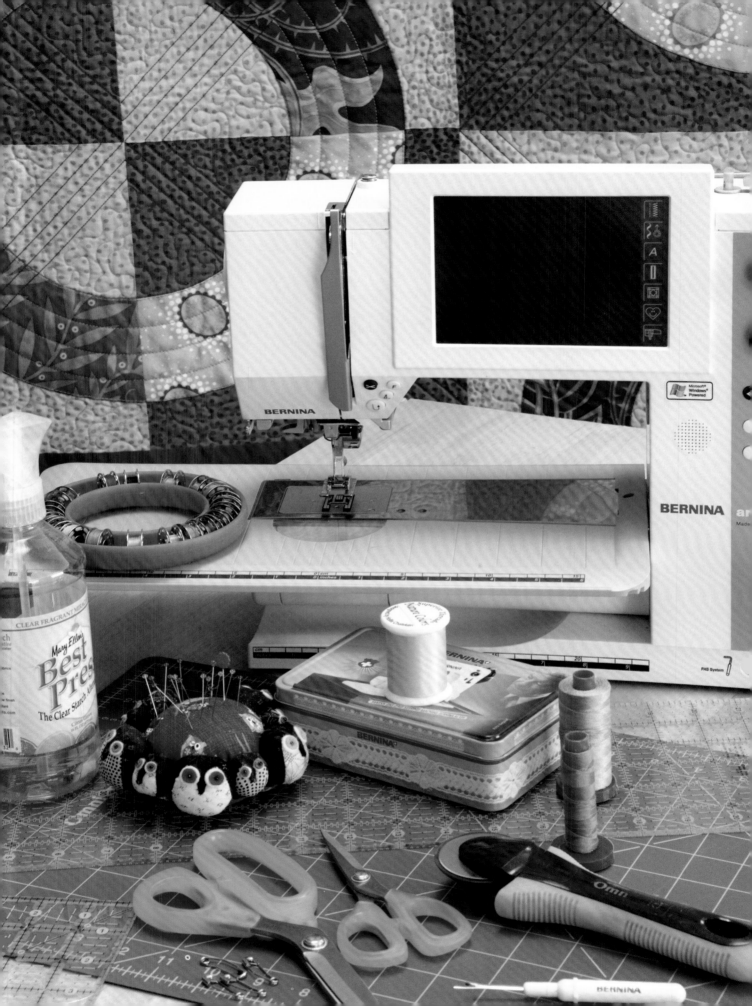

Quilting has become very sophisticated over the last thirty years and there seems to be a tool for any situation. But if you are just getting started, here are the things that will serve you well on your quilting adventure. Most of these tools are also everyday domestic tools, so you are probably halfway there already.

Sewing machine

A reliable sewing machine is a necessity. Without a machine you can depend on, you will be frustrated and discouraged. This doesn't mean you need the latest model or the top of the line…but that sure is fun! Many older machines, if properly maintained, can last a lifetime. So before you get started you may want to get your machine cleaned and tuned for your carefree sewing enjoyment. For the patterns shown in this book, you will need a machine with a nice straight stitch and a zigzag.

Sewing machine needles and thread

There are sewing machine needles and threads for every fabric and occasion. For piecing I use regular cotton or cotton/poly sewing thread on the top of the machine and in the bobbin. Use a 70/10 microtex needle with that.

For embroidery and satin stitch I use regular sewing thread or a slightly heavier embroidery thread (30 wt. is nice) on top and a matching color of regular thread in the bobbin. An embroidery needle works well for this.

If I have the luxury of quilting one of my tops, I like to use heavy topstitching thread (12wt) in the top of the machine and a matching color of regular thread in the bobbin. A 14 or 16 topstitching needle works best for this thick thread, along with a nice long stitch.

But many of these pieces have been quilted by some talented longarm quilters. Their help has been invaluable and has enabled me to get on with preparations for trade shows, etc. Longarm quilting can not use the same heavy threads that I prefer, but most of my quilters have experimented with different threads and thread combinations to create a thicker line of stitching to mimic the look that I like.

Quilting Foot

Most sewing machines come with interchangeable feet for specific uses. And many have a quilting (piecing) foot which makes it easier to sew a consistent quarter-inch seam, the standard for piecing. I would highly recommend investing in one of these feet. However, if that's not possible, you can mark a quarter-inch on your sewing machine with tape. Use a thin ruler to measure ¼" from the point where your needle touches the fabric and lay your tape parallel to the needle. The more consistent your seams are sewn, the easier your pieces will fit together.

Open-toed Embroidery Foot

For embroidery and satin stitching, an open-toed embroidery foot is wonderful. It allows you to see exactly where the needle is going and makes it easier to control your stitches.

Large Quilting Ruler

A 24" X 6" acrylic quilting ruler with an eighth-inch grid is invaluable. It is also helpful to have 30°, 45° and 60° angles marked. This ruler is heavy enough to hold its position while you cut with your rotary cutter.

Template Plastic

There are many clear acrylic templates in other shapes and sizes with printed grids and measurements available at your quilt store and over time you will accumulate many of them. But often it is still necessary to make your own from semi-transparent sheets of template plastic.

Large Cutting Mat

I recommend a 36" X 24" cutting mat, if you have room. The mat should be self-healing and printed with an all-over 1" grid and quarter-inch notations around the edges. I prefer a mat that has a matte finish instead of a hard shiny finish, as your blade can get a better grip.

Rotary Cutter

A 45 mm. rotary cutter is the workhorse of cutters. They come in small and large sizes, but the 45 mm. will suit most of your quilting needs. A fresh new blade will make your day much easier and your pieces more precise.

Scissors

A quality pair of scissors is a necessity. Of course, there are scissors for every situation, too, but a nice 8" scissor is the place to begin. I also rely on my smaller embroidery scissors for appliqué and detail work.

Iron

Irons are always a topic of conversation among quilters and everyone has their favorites. You can find them for $15 to $300. For basic piecing and quilting, a steam iron is needed. Some require distilled water and most of them are designed to turn themselves off after being unused for a designated period of time. Most dedicated quilters find this last feature very irritating! But many of us have also forgotten to turn off the iron at the end of the day and have been thankful for that feature in the long run. There are some professional irons or steam generators that do not have auto shut-off.

Ironing Surface

A standard ironing board is OK, but I prefer a larger ironing surface, especially when working with large pieces of fabric. You can purchase a "Big Board" which fits on top of your household ironing board and is padded and covered and gives you a 22" X 29" work area. I have also made a portable ironing surface from an old wooden drawing board covered with towels and heat-proof fabric.

Work Wall

The work wall is another new tool adapted by contemporary quilters. This can be portable or permanent and is used for viewing and arranging your quilt pieces. There are some portable work walls available commercially or you can make one from a folding presentation board from the office supply store, or a folding cutting cardboard from your fabric store. Just cover them with white or natural colored cotton flannel. The fuzziness of the flannel will hold your pieces without pins and so rearranging them will be more spontaneous.

Since I have a dedicated quilting room, my work wall is permanent and made from 4' X 8' sheets of foil backed insulation which are covered in poster paper.

Hinged Design Mirror

This simple device is an effective and low tech way to view the kaleidoscope possibilities in your fabrics.

Iron-on Interfacing

I use iron-on interfacing for appliqué and broderie perse. Each shape is backed with interfacing, as is the background. The interfacing acts as a stabilizer for the embroidery and quilting to follow.

Fusible Web

Fusible web is a double-sided adhesive which is activated by the heat of an iron. It works like glue to permanently adhere appliqué pieces to a background.

Starch Substitute

Seamstresses have been using starch to stiffen and strengthen fabrics for ages. Traditionally made from cornstarch and water, it often flaked when ironed and was susceptible to insects, if not thoroughly washed out. Today there is a wonderful starch alternative which is clear and easy to use. Also, it is acid-free and not attractive to bugs.

Cutting Fabric

Fabric is made of threads that are woven in two directions and at right angles (A). Consequently, we want to take advantage of this characteristic when we cut our fabric shapes for piecing.

This means that we want to cut with the "straight of the grain" whenever possible. In Example B, two sides of the triangle are cut with the grain. However, the long side of the triangle is a "bias" cut. When the fabric is cut on a bias, the shape is less stable and stretching can easily occur. Therefore, we need to handle these pieces with care so they keep their shape. We can also treat the fabric with spray starch or starch substitute (my preference) to stiffen the fabric, thus helping it to hold its shape.

In Example C, the long edge is cut with the straight of the grain and the short sides are cut on the bias. Both examples are correct; it just depends which direction you want the fabric's print to go.

In this book we have many examples of "fussy cutting" or cutting fabric to feature a specific area. This means we are often cutting bias cuts, so please treat these fabrics with spray starch substitute before cutting and handle these shapes with special care.

The more precisely your shapes are cut, the easier it will be to piece them together accurately.

fussy cutting

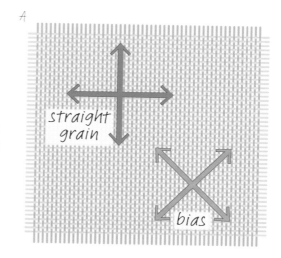

A

straight grain

bias

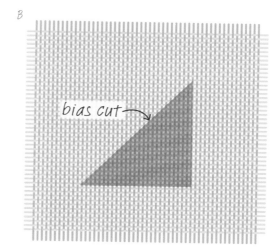

B

bias cut

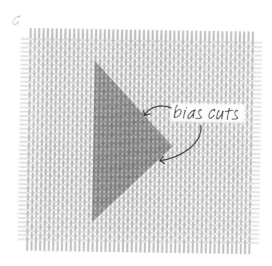

C

bias cuts

Pressing vs. ironing

In patchwork it is important to "press" your pieces as opposed to "ironing" them. Yes, you will have to iron (drag in a long motion) your fabrics after you wash them. But as you are piecing with smaller shapes, pressing with a gentle up and down motion will help keep your blocks in shape.

As you assemble your blocks, you will need to press as you go and make your seams lay one way or the other. One rule of thumb is to press the seams toward the darkest fabric. This assures that the dark fabric will not show or shadow through the lighter fabric. This is also helpful when nesting rows of pieced

blocks together, like in this nine-patch. Nesting means that the seams of one pieced unit fit snugly with the seams of its neighbor. This creates clean corners and continuous lines in your block.

When all the rows are sewn together, I press the final seams open.

However, sometimes there isn't any chance of the dark fabric showing through (if all your fabrics are dark, for example). In this case it makes sense for all the seams to alternate directions from one row to the next.

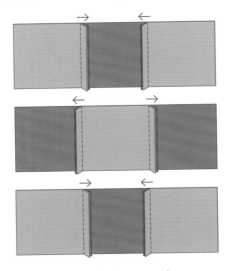

dark and light 9-patch

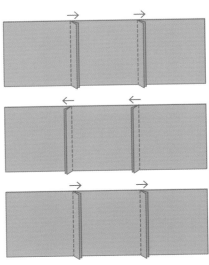

single value 9-patch

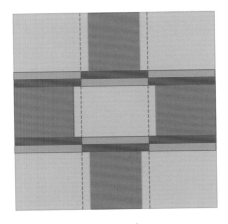

final seams pressed open

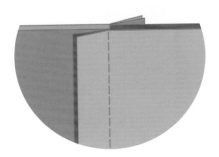

nested seams

Mitered corners

Cut your border strips the length of your top plus double the width of your strips and then add a couple more inches just to be safe.

Center the border strip on the edge of your quilt top, so there are equal amounts hanging over each end.

Pin in place.

Begin stitching ¼" from the corner of the top and stopping ¼" from the end of the top. Tie or backstitch at both ends for security.

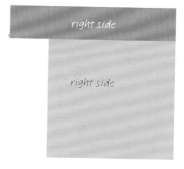

Flip border up and press seams towards border.

Repeat this process on all the other sides.

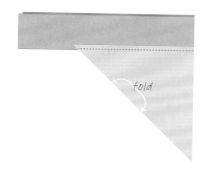

Fold your quilt diagonally so two perpendicular sides line up. This will create a 45° wedge, with the border strips running off the end.

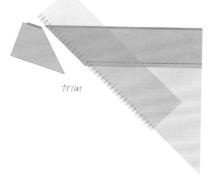

Line your folded fabric with the ¼" mark on your ruler and rotary cut through the border strips.

Stitch the strips together using a ¼" seam.

Press the seam open, repeat for each corner.

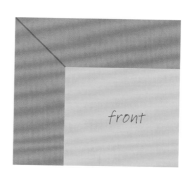

In each of these quilt patterns you will find several variations of the same idea and as you study the quilts you will notice that many are made with deliberately cut pieces of fabric to create special effects such as kaleidoscope and mirror image.

There are three basic ways to cut fancy fabrics: random cuts, fussy cuts and mirror cuts.

1. Random Cuts

A random cut means that you are cutting the piece from any part of the fabric without reference to its printed design. This cut is very effective for fabrics with small motifs, printed fabrics that read as a solid color, or fabrics without a definite direction in their design.

If you are random cutting 10" blocks, for example, you would cut a strip of fabric the width of your finished block plus seam allowance (10½") and cut that strip into as many 10½" squares as possible.

2. Fussy Cuts

A fussy cut means that you are cutting your fabric to take advantage of a specific motif, color or direction of the fabric design. For example, if you want a medallion in the center of your quilt, you may want to cut out the fabric so the motif is nicely centered. Or you may want to repeat a square of a specific section, as in the One + Four Patch recipe quilt. In this case, determine the size of your block and mark your template with registration marks, so the design will line up in the same place for each block cut.

registration marks on template

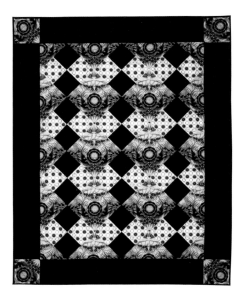

3. Mirror Cuts

Mirror cuts are also fussy cuts, but in this case they are used to exploit the inherent possibilities of fabric with symmetrical designs. Since many of my fabrics have symmetrical prints, you will notice lots of fussy mirror cuts in this book.

The special effects from mirror cuts are some of the most entertaining and surprising results when working with symmetrical designs. Here are a few examples of mirror cuts. Note that all of the motifs are centered.

Now let's multiply those fussy shapes and begin to play.

Another possibility is pairing the same cuts but using two different colorways of the same fabric. The motifs still blend and create movement, but the background makes an alternating and secondary pattern for different graphic effects.

All of the previous examples used a perfectly symmetrical motif, but you can also fussy cut an asymmetrical design for dramatic movement and kaleidoscopic effect.

Design Aids

High Tech Fabric Play

If you have some basic computer knowledge, a digital camera or scanner and a design program, like Adobe Photoshop Elements, Corel Draw or Electric Quilt, you can play with your fabrics' potential digitally before you commit to cutting.

I am familiar with Photoshop from my years as a fabric designer, so this is what I use if I want to get a sneak peek at a new idea before I start slicing into my yardage. My knowledge of Photoshop grows a little each year but I am a long way from being an expert. Obviously, the more you use a program the more familiar and comfortable you become. It takes time and practice to learn a new software. But if I can learn it, so can you. It is wonderful, too, to have a friend that can walk you through the basics and that you can go to for technical advice. There are very good online classes, tutorials and support sites for all the software mentioned above.

No matter which software you use, you still have to get the fabric images into your computer. I always begin by isolating real sized shapes (squares, triangle, diamonds, etc.) by cutting windows (the size of the finished shape) in poster board and laying the window over my fabric. This way I am assured that all the shapes will be in proportion to each other and show the actual part of the fabric design that I want to use. Then I take a photograph of each one and bring them into Photoshop. In Photoshop I can rearrange and experiment. I can add and subtract fabrics and test lots of colors and compositions before pledging my allegiance to a less than ideal design.

You can also physically cut out your initial fabric shapes and copy them on a scanner. But many of my cuts are larger than the bed of my scanner, which means I'd need to take the time to piece them digitally together. The other disadvantage of using a scanner with fabric is the interesting, yet annoying, moire pattern created by the weave of the cloth. But nonetheless a scanner is a valid way to transfer an image of your fabric into your computer.

Low Tech Fabric Play

However, I usually prefer to design the "old fashioned" way. Nothing beats fondling fabric and playing with your quilting tools. I so enjoy the excitement of hunting down the right fabric for a perfect solution that cutting some experimental shapes is just part of the fun.

While making the quilts in this book there were a few quilting tools that were used again and again to help make my fabric choices and assist in constructing the quilt.

hinged mirror

Since there are so many symmetrical fussy cut fabrics featured in these pages, the hinged mirror tool has been invaluable. The hinged mirrors are used to preview the kaleidoscopic potential of a fabric design, especially fabrics with symmetrical patterns. Ideally, the mirrors should be heavy plastic and bound with a flexible tape hinge at one end. I am usually cutting large pieces of fabric, so I appreciate a large set of mirrors to view bigger areas of pattern.

You can adjust the mirrors to any angle and move them over the fabric to find the most effective area to fussy cut. To adjust the degree of angle, use the angle markings on your quilting rulers. I sometimes use white paper to mask the extra fabric from view.

Perfectly engineered rulers are a quilter's delight. You can never have too many. The advantage of commercially made rulers over a self-made template are many. They are sturdy, they last forever and are extremely accurate. The best rulers have precisely printed grids and other markings as helpful cutting guides.

But a nice ruler needs an equally good cutting mat to partner with. The markings on both should sync up absolutely. I have found that it is helpful if both the mat and rulers are made by the same company, since they are scientifically designed to work together.

A Low Tech Way to Figure Yardage

For formal quilt patterns the fabric yardage is usually listed with the instructions. But very often we want to make the quilt with different fabrics than the original. Sometimes this means that the scale of the pieces may have to change, too. If the pieces are fussy cut, as many are in this book, the yardage will need to change, too. How do you know how much fabric you will need?

Each fabric design has its own set of stipulations, for example, the size of the repeat both lengthwise and widthwise and the position of the print on the cloth will affect the number of pieces available to cut out.

Let's say you want to make the One + Four Patch quilt with the Prairie Poppy fabric as the focus patch.

Spread the opened fabric on the floor and look at the repeat. In this case there is a brick type repeat where the motif is reversed in every other row. Your first decision is what size block will be the most effective size. After trying several sizes, I settled on an 8" finished block.

The next thing you need to determine is the direction of the motif since the swirling flowers go two different directions. Is it important that they all bend the same way or could I use flowers going both ways successfully? Obviously, there will be more "swiss cheese" left over if the flowers only lean one way, so I think I will combine the two in alternate rows. "Swiss cheese" is what quilters call the holey fabric left over after fussy-cutting.

So how can I plan for the most cost effective way to cut and how much fabric I will need? Since I know I'm using an 8" square, my template will be 8½". Place your template over your material and determine the exact place in the design that you want to cut. If necessary, make simple registration marks to line up with the section you want to cut. I have decided to have the flowers in the blocks alternate by row and I want the block to line up so all the stems are included.

Then I cut six 8½" squares, ten half-square triangles and four quarter-square triangles from scrap paper, since these are all the pieces I will need for the body of the quilt. I will also transfer the registration marks onto these, too. Keep in mind the direction of the

half-square triangles and the quarter-square triangles because the motifs will be a portion of the original.

Lay the paper templates directly over the proper sections of your fabric. Photograph the layout and try rearranging again until you have the most efficient cutting plan. This means that you are using the least amount of fabric as possible.

Is there enough fabric to cut the four corner squares amongst the "swiss cheese"? If not, add these blocks to the yardage. Photograph your arrangement, just in case the cat disturbs it. You can pin the paper patterns loosely to your fabric and move the yardage to your cutting board to make the perfect cuts using your original clear templates.

I also think I'd like to have the four-patch block made with a yellow and green tone-on-tone print. Since these fabrics don't have a specific direction in their print, I can simply cut 4½" strips of each to make the coordinating blocks. But if they needed fussy-cutting, I could estimate the yardage just as before.

After years of making quilts from "personality prints", I have collected some simple patchwork recipes which I can always depend on. You will see that I have made each of these patterns several times in different sizes and fabrics. So just like a recipe in the kitchen, these patchwork recipes are flexible. They can be adjusted according to your taste and the ingredients at hand. In this case our ingredients are big, bold beautiful printed fabrics.

The recipes progress in complexity by chapter, beginning with an almost "whole cloth" quilt and gradually evolving to a large "broken star" design and even some appliqué. Each chapter adds a new patchwork element, so we can gently guide you through the basic concepts of quilt design and construction.

Every chapter also gives at least two interpretations of each pattern. You might be amazed by the radical differences between some of them. But in each case, the fabric dictates the direction a quilt takes. So throughout these pages I will encourage you to let the fabric be your guide. The simple geometry of patchwork lends a bit of discipline and order to a composition made with an exuberant textile.

All of these recipes are technically easy to make, although sometimes they may look quite the opposite. But the complexity is in the fabric and how you use it, not in the construction. By learning to listen to the character of your cloth you can make your own unique quilts with very little labor.

So begin with the first recipe and absorb some patchwork skills one step at a time. At the end of this "cookbook" you will know all the basics for whipping up some dazzling quilts with your own fabulous fabrics.

Wall vs Bed

One of the most wonderful results of designing fabric are the varied and unexpected quilts that have evolved from them. Unlike my appliquéd art quilts, which can take months to make, my large scale printed fabrics have allowed me to make larger quilts in a much shorter amount of time. First, because the fabric takes the place of the appliqué, my motifs are printed already and this allows me to focus on the character of the print. Also, large prints are meant to be enjoyed as a whole, not cut into little pieces, so the piecing is very easy and the fabric does most of the work.

But speed doesn't mean you have to sacrifice beauty or drama. The smaller investment of time has allowed me to let some of my new quilts become "utility" quilts, which would never happen with my precious appliquéd pieces. So these new quilts can still be stunners, except the fabric is doing the lion's share of the work instead of the maker.

Every quilt in this book is suited for hanging on the wall, but many of them are also large enough to use as a throw or to cover a bed. However, rarely do I design a quilt to be used specifically on a bed. I allow a quilt to grow or shrink during the design process and if it grows large enough to cover a bed, then that's a bonus. Consequently, the quilts in this book are not built around bed sizes, although they can all be adjusted for that purpose if you desire.

My objective when designing a quilt is to simply make the best quilt I can with the fabric at hand.

The complexity is in the fabric and how you use it, not in the construction. By learning to listen to the character of your cloth you can make your own unique quilts with very little labor.

Amish Bars

After the basic Whole Cloth quilt, the next evolution is to break the body of the quilt into stripes or bars. An Amish Bars design is essentially alternating colors of vertical stripes which fill a large central block. Sometimes the block is surrounded by a wide single border or a sashing and a border. Amish Bars is sometimes called "Joseph's Coat" from the well-known "coat of many colors" in the Bible.

This is a design that I have used several times for the back of a more complicated piece. After all, a quilt has two sides and it seems a shame not to take advantage of both of them. Two quilts in one!

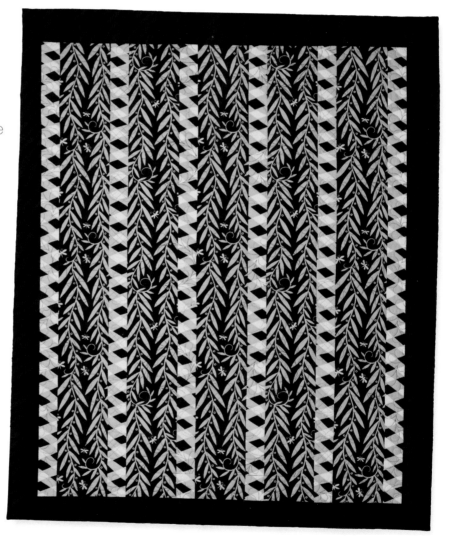

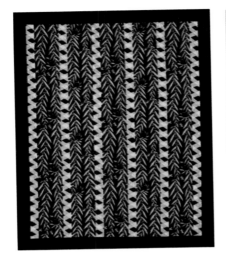
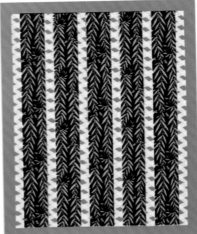
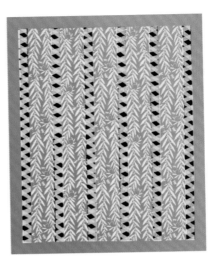

Notice in the sample quilts that the strips shown have a color in common with each other. Also see that the wide strip is made from a more complicated print and the narrow one has a simpler pattern. Also one strip is light and his neighbor is dark. So these fabrics are contrasting, yet coordinating.

Audition your fabrics by folding them into lengths and setting them next to each other. Keep auditioning until you find the right combination.

Next you will want to determine the size of your strips, how wide and how long. The width of your strips may be determined by the width of the printed pattern. This is a very individual decision. Once the size of the strips has been determined, cut them out, including the quarter-inch seam allowance. Pin the alternating strips on your work wall and arrange them according to your desired look.

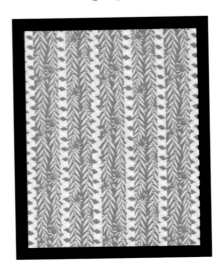

Next you need to audition your border fabric. The border acts as a frame. The Amish Bars "recipe" quilt has just a simple black border to frame the center strips, which is quite striking because the two strip fabrics share the color black, too.

Sew all your bars together and press all the seams toward the darkest fabric. Square off the block of strips, if needed.

Cut two border strips the length of your strips and stitch to opposite sides. Press seams toward the border.

Cut two more strips the length of the remaining two sides. Stitch and press.

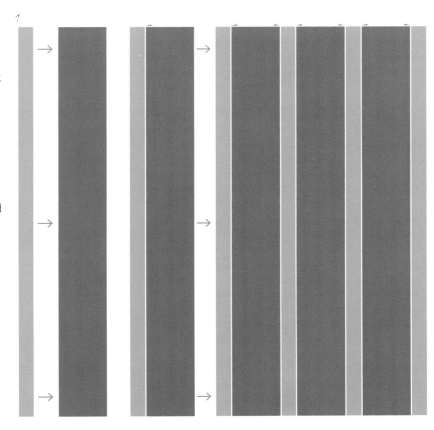

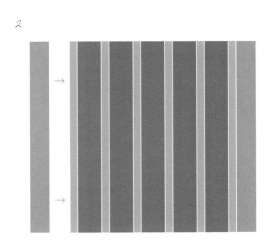

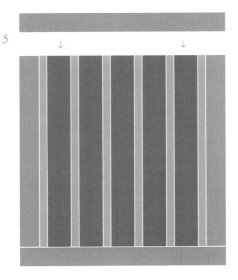

In the Amish Bars gallery, however, there are several variations of this design. These two have both a mat and a frame which can act just like the mat and frame of the "whole cloth" recipe in the last chapter.

They also have corner blocks in the border. Corner squares are a traditional quilt element which you will encounter as we progress through the recipes.

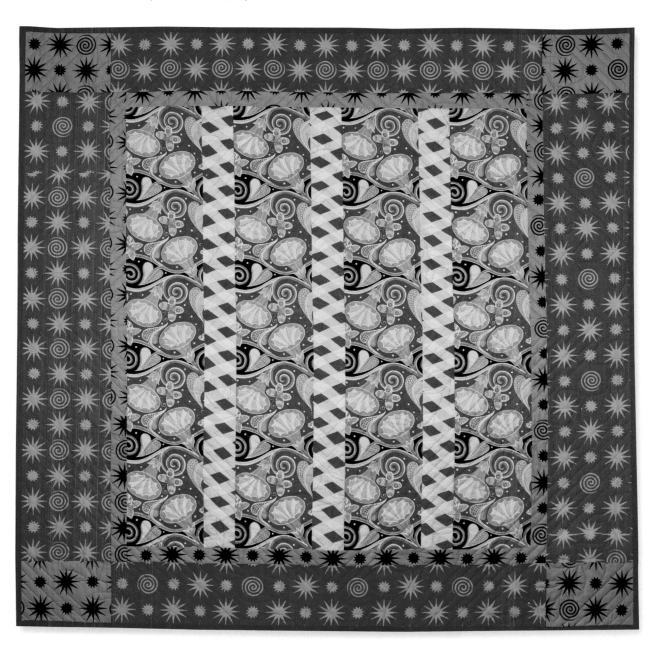

Circus Bars

After you determine the size of your feature block, make three templates for your feature fabric: one whole block with seam allowance, one half-square triangle with seam allowance and one quarter-square triangle with seam allowance. Because the feature blocks are cut on the diagonal, care must be taken to prevent too much stretching. It will help to spritz your feature fabric with a starch substitute before ironing and cutting. This will add a little extra stiffness and strength. The four-patch block, however, has been cut with the straight of grain and will be a little less delicate.

Cut 6 fussy on-point blocks from your stiffened feature fabric. You may need to mark your template with registration marks so you can accurately cut the same part of the design over and over again.

Next we will cut the half-square triangles. I find it very helpful to use a whole block as my guide. Fold the block in half and lay it on top of the fabric so the designs match. Lay your half-square template exactly over the block (the template will be a little bigger than the folded block because it includes the necessary seam allowance) and carefully slip the folded block away. Now you know exactly where to cut.

If you put all your blocks on your work wall, it will be easier to keep track of which pieces need to be cut. Now repeat the process for the quarter-square triangles in the corner.

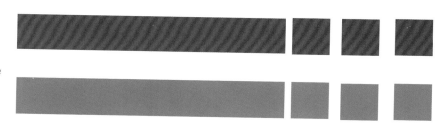

Rotary cut 4 ½" strips of your two 4-patch fabrics and cut those strips into 4 ½" squares

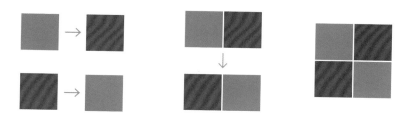

To make four-square blocks sew together pairs of lights and darks.

The four-patch blocks are made with squares that are quarter-size of the whole block with seam allowances added. In our sample quilt, these are 4" finished (4½" with seam allowance).

The easiest way to cut these blocks is to rotary cut 4½" strips of your two 4-patch fabrics and cut those strips into 4½" squares. Just use your large clear quilting ruler, no need to make a template.

The four-square blocks create a checkerboard with light and dark fabrics. To make these blocks, sew together pairs of lights and darks.

Press to set the seams, then open and press the seams toward the dark fabric. Now place two pairs with right sides and opposite colors together, nest the seams, pin and stitch. Set the seams, and press open.

Now you have all the pieces to make the body of the quilt. It will be constructed in rows, but the rows lay diagonally since the blocks are on point.

Begin at the top left corner and assemble one row at a time. Press all seams toward the feature fabric. After all rows are made, sew the rows together, being sure to nest the seams. As each successive row is added, set and press the seams open.

Use your rotary cutter and ruler to cut the border strips. Depending on the size of your quilt top, these strips can be pieced together if they are too short.

Cut the long side borders the same size as the long sides of the quilt body and cut two the same length as the short sides. Cut four corner squares the same width. Pin the two long sides first, stitch, set seam, press seams open and press toward the border fabric.

Sew the corner blocks to the ends of the remaining strips and press the seams toward the border fabric. Pin, stitch, set and press the seams toward the border.

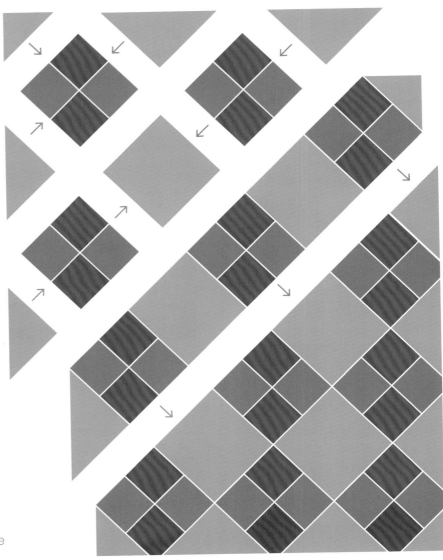

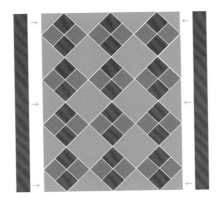

Morning Song

The "feature" blocks in this variation are filled with several fussy cut motifs from the same fabric, as opposed to cutting the exact motif over and over again. The four-patch blocks in this quilt also create strong horizontal rows of pink squares, whereas the original quilt emphasizes vertical rows of black.

Checkerboard Plaid

Although this quilt is very easy to piece, the graphic effects can be quite sophisticated. The body of the quilt uses three fancy fabrics arranged in a gingham pattern of light, medium and dark. Each square is fussy cut to create an interweaving or blending relationship with its neighbor. There is also a secondary diagonal pattern.

To select your block fabrics look for obvious repeats with radial symmetry (bull's eye) in coordinated colors and in light, medium and dark values. Often, you can stay within a single designer's collection to make your selection.

The surrounding sashing focuses the checks and creates a frame. The border and corner squares add the finishing touch. The border measurement is the same width as the center block.

First you need to audition the three fabrics for your center blocks. You may want to make a simple viewing window from a sheet of paper to help isolate the most effective sections of the fabric design.

Just use scratch paper and cut a square out of the middle. You could even make these in several sizes to test which block size will work best for your fabrics. Lay the paper on your fabric and move it around until you find the symmetrical portion that you like.

Cut a few test blocks and use your work wall to help you make final fabric choices and arrangements. Your rows will alternate between rows of light and medium and rows of dark and medium squares. Again, the size of your block depends on the size of your print. In the sample quilt the block is 6" square and the fabrics are cut so that part of the design is cropped off. This cropping allows the colors to blend with its neighbors.

Since these three fabrics are all fussy cut, it will be easiest to make a template to cut the squares. Determine the size of the square and add your seam allowance to all sides for your template. Then add registration marks for more accurate cutting.

Cut and rearrange the blocks on your wall. Now you can audition the border fabrics. The skinny inner border is a transition between the body of the quilt and the outer border, so it needs to coordinate with both. In every example, I have chosen a fabric with a clean and simple pattern for the slim border to harmonize with, yet define, the body of the quilt.

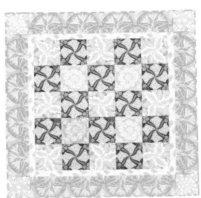

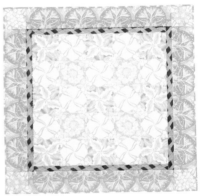

For the outer border or final frame, I have picked a coordinating fabric with lots of personality of its own. This only works, however, because the style of the print echoes the feeling and is in a similar design style to the other fabrics. These prints also have a definite rhythm which finishes the quilt with elegance and formality.

The corner blocks are repeated from the fabrics in the body of the quilt.

Again, you can probably work within the same collection, but I encourage you to mix and match for more exciting results.

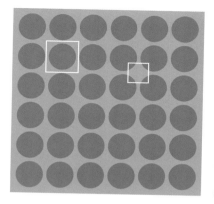 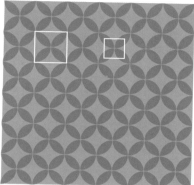 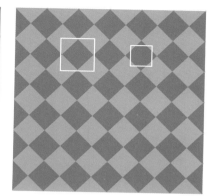

Fussy cropping

For this quilt, fussy cutting, or cropping your fabric is very important. In fact, what you don't see is almost as important as what you do see. As we mentioned in previous chapters, a border can focus the subject it surrounds. The same is true when cropping a design because the sides stop the picture. But in this case, we want each block to blend a bit with its neighbor. This means they each need to have something in common, especially on the

border where they touch each other. They can share common colors, textures or shapes.

So if you crop your motif so it is floating in the middle of the block there will be nothing to connect to the square next door. But by cropping "inside" the motif you allow the blocks to touch and blend.

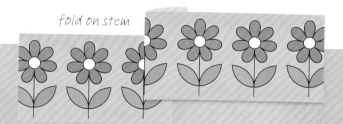

fold on stem

Piecing borders

If your border has an obvious repeat, like these, any interruption of the pattern would be disturbing, so be sure you are cutting the same part of the design for each row. Notice, too, that each border strip is centered on each side. If your quilt is longer than the length of your border fabric, you will need to piece strips together so the pattern looks continuous and the joins don't show.

I have a little trick for doing this. Lay two strips on your ironing board and examine them for the most economical place to piece them together. This just means you want to waste as little fabric as possible. Then fold one of the fabrics on the motif

that will match up with its other half. Try to pick the least noticeable place like a perpendicular stem, if possible. Line them up perfectly and press the fold.

Carefully lift the folded edge so you don't disturb either strip. Then run a tiny bead of fabric glue along the inner edge of the fold. Lay it carefully down again and press. Let it dry and trim the extra fabric away.

Turn the strip over and stitch in the ditch of the fold.

Begin by sewing the center blocks together, one row at a time. Start at the top and press all seams toward the darkest fabric. Then stitch the rows together, nesting the seams carefully.

The sashing, as always, is added to two opposite sides first, with the seams pressed toward the sashing. Then attach the sashing to the remaining sides. Cut 4 border strips the length and width of the quilt top and 4 corner square blocks the same width.

Sew on the two opposite sides and press seams toward the border. Attach the corner blocks to each end of the remaining border strips and press seams toward the border. Pin and stitch these final pieces. Press seams open.

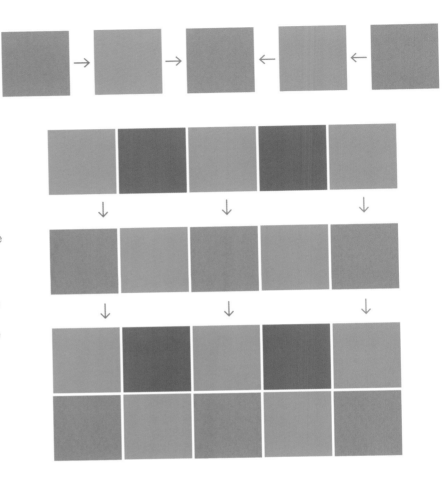

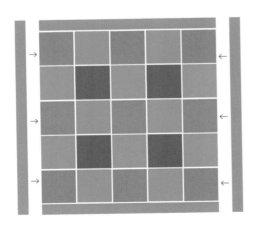

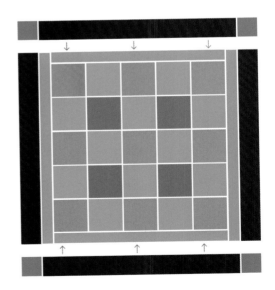

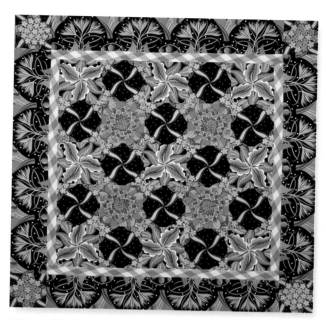

Floral Fantasy in Blue

In the variation quilts, you will see that the same quilt has been done in three colorways of the same fabric. The position of the dark and light blocks are shifted but the three values are still there. This is a possibility that you should keep in mind. Very often simply shifting to another colorway within the same fabric collection will be just as effective as the "original" quilt. Never limit yourself to someone else's pattern if you think you can make it better.

Floral Fantasy in Red

Dragonfly Moon

Dragonfly Moon actually combines two colorways of the same fabric. One acts as the dark block, the other as a light one. The moons in the third block have been fussy cut in half, creating an "X" in the negative space. The severed moon motif blends into the neighboring blocks for a stunning graphic effect.

Radiating Diamonds

The Radiating Diamonds pattern can result in some amazing quilts and it all happens because the squares are set on-point and act as fingers that interlace with its neighbor. This is a very nice pattern for blending fabrics by color and texture. It lends itself to symmetrical prints, but is by no means dependent on them. Often, you can rely on a single designer's line to supply all the fabrics for this quilt because this is how most collections are also organized…coordinated colors and patterns in many scales.

This is one of those quilt patterns that has so many possibilities. I do lots of experimentation and cut many sample blocks before making my decisions. But these blocks are never wasted! They make good beginnings for a second quilt, pillows and other projects along the way.

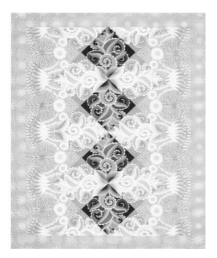

I like to begin with a medallion print for the center squares (A), or the spine of the quilt. The size of the medallion will determine the size of the block. Notice that the design is cropped, as opposed to floating in the middle of the block. The cropped elements are always the bridges to the next row of fabrics since they actually touch each other.

The next two rows are made from the same fussy cut motif and are arranged so they mirror image each other. This can make some extraordinary kaleidoscopic effects. Add half-square triangles (B) to the ends of the rows.

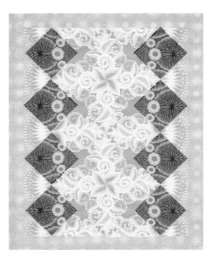

The next row of blocks (C) requires a fabric that echoes some of the same colors as the original fabric, except in different proportions. This is where the blending begins. In this case, the yellow/orange lilies make a smooth bridge from the reds and oranges in the *Tree of Life* print. Plus all the other colors in the new block are also in the original block.

Then our sample quilt has a row of half-square triangles (D) for the next layer of transition. Again the fabrics repeat the green, gold and red from before. The arch of gold also mimics the previous arch of gold lilies.

Quarter-square triangles (E) fill in the corners.

The border was chosen to blend in with the triangles and to tie in with the center blocks again.

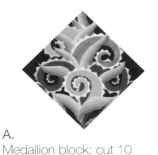

A.
Medallion block: cut 10

B.
Half-square medallion: cut 4

C.
Side block: cut 8

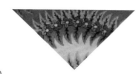

D.
Half-square triangle: cut 6

E.
Quarter-square triangle: cut 4

Make your template for the basic square and its half-square and quarter-square triangles.

Cut 10 medallion squares (A) and pin them on your work wall so they mirror each other.

Next determine the half-square triangle medallions (B) you will need to finish the top and bottom.

I find it very helpful to use a whole block as my guide. Fold the block in half and lay it on top of the fabric so the designs match.

Lay your half-square template exactly over the block (the template will be a little bigger than the folded block because it includes the necessary seam allowance) and carefully slip the folded block away. Now you know exactly where to cut.

Audition your next fabric for the side blocks (C) and fussy cut 8 of the same block. Pin them to your work wall.

Audition the next fabrics for the side half-square triangles (D) then cut 6 of these and 4 quarter-square triangles (E).

tip:

One way to conserve fabric is to photograph or scan some fabric squares and play with them on your computer to weed through some of the possibilities before committing yourself with the rotary cutter.

You can also play with the direction of your blocks which will give your piece different movement and rhythm. I always end up with several tops when I set out to make this design.

Stitch the blocks together in diagonal rows, as you did for the One + Four Patch Recipe.

Press the seams all in one direction in the first row and press them in the opposite direction in the next row. Continue to alternate as you assemble the rows.

Now the rows will be sewn together beginning with a corner. Pin the first two together, being sure to nest your seams and stitch. Press the seam open. Repeat for all rows.

Rotary cut your border strips and cut two the same length as your quilt top. Pin and stitch. Press seams toward the border.

Cut two strips the width of your top. Pin and stitch. Press toward the border fabric.

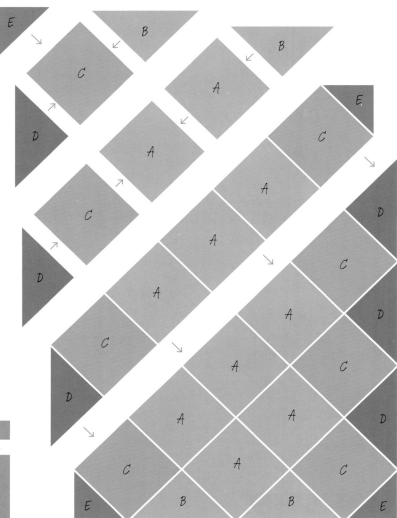

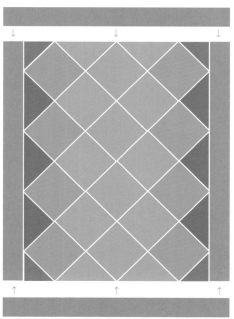

Oriental Carpet

Oriental Carpet is a more complicated version of this recipe. It has more interlacing blocks of fabric and a very sophisticated weaving of colors, pattern and texture. But each row still mimics a color from its neighbor. I chose, too, to miter the corners to carry through the "zigzag" composition.

This kind of quilt is a collage which evolves a row at a time. And it is always a surprising adventure. I find this way of working very satisfying because there are creative decisions to make every step of the way. The final product is always a delightful surprise.

Fancy Nine-Patch

The Fancy Nine-Patch is a variation of the classic Nine-Patch quilt block. The Nine-Patch is simply a block made of nine squares—three rows of three. Traditionally this block is arranged so the colors create a cross.

In this recipe we have magnified the block to fill the entire body of the quilt. But we have also divided each patch into four fussy-cut mirror image squares. Each square in the block is cut on-point to take advantage of the kaleidoscopic potential of symmetrical prints.

The delicate sample quilt also mimics the traditional nine-patch by alternating light and dark blocks for a cross, or checkerboard, composition. Both light and dark blocks share colors in common, yet the dark blocks look lacy and the light blocks are more open and plain. This contrast in textures helps to define each block, while the shared colors blend them together. These fabrics are also related by subject or theme, as they both have butterfly motifs. These surprising interactions are what make kaleidoscope quilts so entertaining. Where does one block end and the other begin?

The center of this quilt was so much fun to look at and has so much going on that I chose a solid green fabric for the sashing. It helps to confine the activity, but it is also the transition to the border. The border is made of the same fabric as the dark blocks and the corner squares are the same as the light ones. I thought it would be nice to see the original fabrics before they had been altered.

Audition your fabrics. Look for similar colors, but in different proportions, and perhaps a common subject matter. Determine the size of your square according to the size of the fabric motifs. Remember that four squares make a block. Use your hinged mirror tool to find the most effective repeat.

Remember, too, the edge is shared by both fabrics, so this is the transition line. Don't be afraid to crop part of a motif so the edges can interact to heighten the kaleidoscopic effects.

Cut sixteen squares of one fabric and twenty of the other. Since these are all bias cuts, use starch substitute to stabilize them.

Arrange them on your work wall, as planned, alternating light and dark blocks. Just for fun, try reversing the squares in your blocks. Sometimes this new arrangement is even better than the original. Try different kaleidoscopic combinations until you find the one you like best.

Audition your sashing.

In this recipe we are simply repeating the body fabrics in the border and corner squares. The border is the same width as your inner squares, so you can cut strips of border now, too. Again, the edge is a transition, so cut for the best result.

The corner squares are also the same width, but from the other fabric. Cut and pin all the pieces to your work wall.

Just for fun, try reversing the squares in your blocks. Sometimes this new arrangement is even better than the original. Try different kaleidoscopic combinations until you find the one you like best.

As always we will construct the body of the quilt first. Assemble each four-square block by sewing pairs (two squares) together and pressing all the seams in the same direction. Nesting all the seams, stitch the pairs together to make your blocks.

Before you press the seams, lay each open block on your table in its proper order. Notice which seams face right and which face left. Now rotate the blocks so the seams will nest. Then press the center seams to finish this formula.

Assemble one row at a time and press the seams toward the dark fabric. Now sew the rows to each other and press the final seams open.

Cut two strips of sashing the same length as the body of your quilt. Sew them to opposite sides and press seams toward the sashing. Cut two more sashing strips the length of the remaining sides, stitch and press as before.

Audition the placement of your borders. You probably want them centered, in keeping with the symmetry of the quilt's center. Then cut four border strips the length of your quilt top. Attach the two opposite side borders first, press seams toward the borders.

Sew a corner block to both ends of the remaining border strips. Press seams toward the border. Sew on these strips, nesting the corner seams, stitch and press.

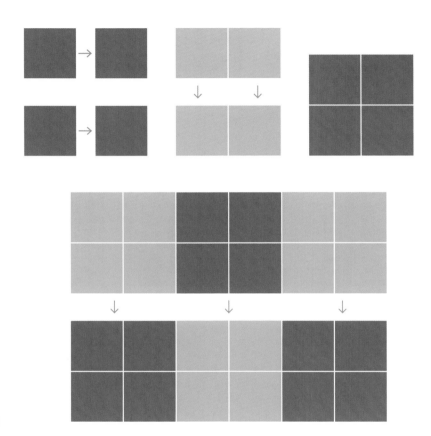

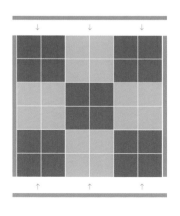

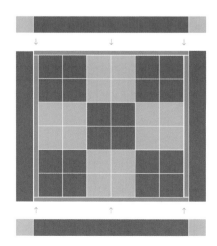

Midnight Coneflowers

In this variation of the Fancy Nine-Patch, all remain the same except for the extra "bug" border. It is the consistant black background that ties the piece together. In fact, this quilt looks almost like a whole cloth quilt because the blacks blend the fabrics together so well.

Cross-in-a-Square

Cross-in-a-Square is exactly like the Fancy Nine-Patch except for the sashing strips. Here the four squares that make up each block are divided by sashing strips with a setting square in the center. Plus each of these blocks is separated from one another by more sashing strips and setting squares. In this sample quilt, all the sashing is the same width but changes color according to its position. I love the interweaving pattern of lines and colors in this recipe. It has a very satisfying sense of order.

In this quilt the light blocks are made of fussy-cut diagonal squares and the dark blocks are random cut. Each light block has a coordinated striped sashing with a black setting square. The dark blocks have black sashing with light setting squares. So there is a system of organization here. All the blocks have both light and dark values to help them communicate with each other.

The sashing that separates each block is light with a black setting square. Black is sprinkled thoughout the quilt and carried into the border for continuity. The border is a frame that directs your eye inward and the blacks tie it all together.

Just as with the Fancy Nine-Patch, audition your block fabrics. Choose fabrics that share common colors, but in different proportions. Choose the size of your square according to the scale of your fabrics.

As in the last chapter, cut 16 squares of one fabric and 20 of the other. Pin these squares to your wall in the same alternating checkerboard pattern, but leave space for the sashing strips. There will be lots of testing and decisions to make. This is when your work wall is invaluable.

In our sample quilt the sashing is always the same width, ¼ the measurement of the square. For example, if you have a 6" finished block, the sashing will be 1½" finished.

Cut strips of various inner sashing candidates and pin them between the light squares and dark squares until you find the winners.

Next test the outer sashing between these blocks. This is the sashing which runs throughout the quilt. Keep testing until you are happy. The little setting squares are always the opposite value of the sashing; light on dark and dark on light. Gradually the quilt will come together.

Now try out some borders. In this case I chose the *Sunflower* fabric again (in the light blocks) but in a different colorway with a black background. The black border helps to unify the quilt.

The corner squares match the sashing. The moth appliqué speaks to the midwestern flora and fauna which inspired this fabric line called *Prairie Gothic*.

Feature fabric squares are cut on bias.

Inner sashing

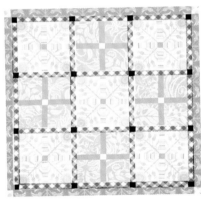

Outer sashing

Border

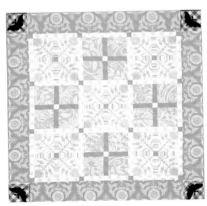

Appliquéd corner squares

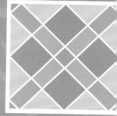

Cross-in-a-Diamond

This design has lots of energy between the diagonal crosses and the alternating light and dark blocks. It is very similar to the previous Cross-in-a-Square recipe, except these blocks are set on-point and are not divided by sashing strips. The three-piece sashing that remains creates the crosses in the middle.

In our sample quilt, none of the pieces have been fussy cut. For this design we are relying on the contrast of the light and dark fabrics to define the blocks. So all the fabrics here have been randomly cut.

Choose a main fabric which has both light and dark colorways and have some colors in common. When determining the size of your basic square, be sure it is large enough to include plenty of background (light or dark).

When considering your triple sashing, look for a coordinating fabric to make a dark cross in the light blocks and a light cross in the dark blocks. For the center stripe, which is consistent throughout the quilt, choose a color with some contrast or electricity. The combined sashing strips are half the width of your basic square (6" finished square = 3" finished sashing).

The setting squares are a consistent color for each block. Choose a fabric which will stand out with both light and dark crosses.

Make a half-square triangle template of your main square. The setting square is the same width as your sashing; make its half-square triangle and quarter-square triangle templates.

Cut selvedge to selvedge strips from both main fabrics that are the width of your unfinished square (6" finished square = 6½" strips).

Cut these strips into squares (6½" squares). Cut 16 dark squares and 8 light squares. Cut 16 light half-square triangles.

From the setting square fabric, cut 5 whole squares, 4 half-square triangles and 4 quarter-square triangles.

Determine the width of your sashing strips (3" strip divided by 3 = 1" strips + seam allowance = 1½" strips). Cut selvedge to selvedge strips of all three sashing fabrics.

Stitch the strips together in dark sets and light sets. Press the seams toward the dark fabrics. Cut these strips into lengths that are the width of your main square (6½" square = 6½" sashing lengths).

Arrange all your pieces on your work wall. Audition the outer sashing strip and border fabrics. Cut strips for the outer sashing that are the same width as the inner sashing. The border is approximately ²/₃ the width of your basic block (6" finished block times ²/₃ = 4" finished border = 4½" cut strips).

Cut sashing strips and border strips.

There are two ways to construct the body of this quilt. You can simply sew it together one diagonal row at a time or sew all your blocks together first and then sew rows of blocks together. In each case, all seams should be pressed toward the dark fabric.

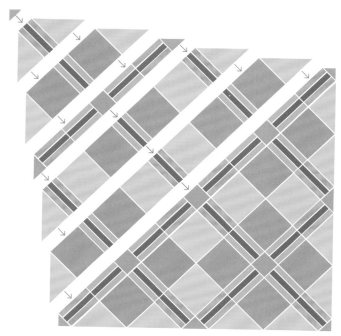

Assemble one diagonal row at a time...

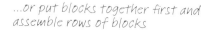

...or put blocks together first and assemble rows of blocks

Assembling the Quilt

When the body of the quilt is completed, cut two outer sashing strips the same length as your quilt body. Stitch them onto opposite sides of your quilt.

Cut two more sashing strips the width of your quilt and attach them to the remaining sides.

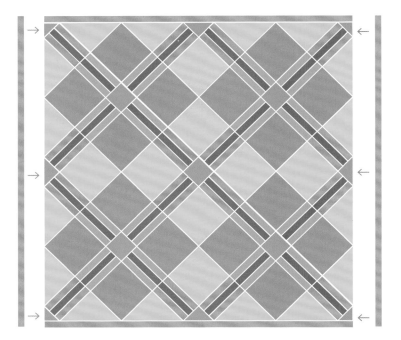

Cut two border strips the same length as your quilt body. Stitch them onto opposite sides of your quilt.

Cut two more border strips the width of your quilt and attach them to the remaining sides. Press seams toward the border.

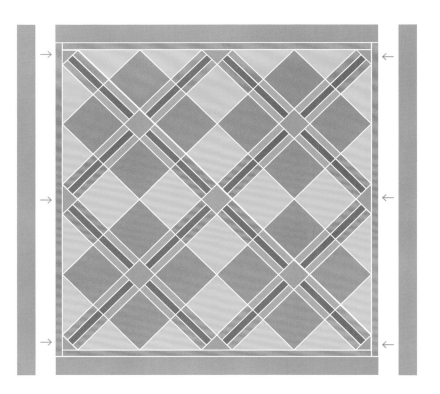

Trading Blanket

I am very fond of this quilt because "he" has such a unique place in this collection. *Trading Blanket* is distinctly masculine; he is sharp and decisive. He reminds me of the very graphic and colorful wool Pendleton blankets from the American Southwest.

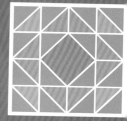

Ocean Waves

Simply by alternating dark, medium and light triangles, the Ocean Waves design creates movement and the illusion of transparency. This is also the first quilt recipe to use blocks made with half-square triangles, almost exclusively.

I like to begin this pattern with a center medallion set on point and surrounded by four dark corners as the large center block. It is equal to the size of four blocks. This block sets the mood or theme of the quilt. The blocks that radiate from the middle are made from triangles of three fabrics. Each block has a dark fabric half and is partnered with a light or medium fabric. The blocks are arranged to create the illusion of alternating stacks of squares.

The sashing contains the energy in the center and creates the mat which separates it from the border. The border makes the frame and also ties the composition back to the middle.

The sample quilt was made with 7" finished blocks, which means the large medallion block is 14" finished. The sashing is 1½" finished and the border is 7" wide finished as well.

Also in this quilt, all the triangle fabrics are random cut, however attention was paid to the direction of the print in the blue and red triangles.

As mentioned before, I like to begin an Ocean Waves quilt with a large interesting print for the center medallion. The light, medium and dark triangles are all related to this original fabric by color. It is also nice to have a variety of textures or scale in these prints, too.

You may have to audition a few possibilities before you have the right combination. Use your work wall for the best viewing. Don't be afraid to cut some real triangles to play with.

Making the Ocean Waves templates

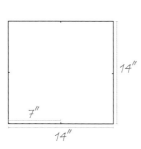
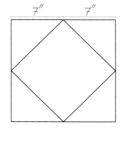

template with seam allowance added

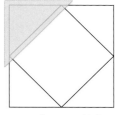

seam allowance added

Make the template for the medallion. Since this quilt is built on a 7" block, the medallion will be 14" in the middle. Draw a 14" square and mark the half way point (7") on all sides. Draw a line connecting these points. Add your seam allowance all the way around for the medallion template.

Now for the triangle template. On the same drawing, take one of the resulting triangles and add the seam allowance around it. Cut both of these out of template plastic.

Lay your medallion template over your central fabric and decide where you'd like to crop the motif. Cut and pin the piece to your wall.

Before you cut your triangles, give some thought about the directions of your prints and how you want them placed in the quilt.

In our sample quilt you will notice that the blue *Willow Wands* fabric is cut so the stems are running diagonally. The checked fabric is also cut with the direction of the design in mind. The direction of the print on the pink fabric is randomly placed.

This means I cut strips of *Willow Wands* fabric a little wider than the height of the triangle to cut the shapes. The straight of grain is on the long edge.

The red and white checks were printed diagonally, so they are on the straight of grain on their two short sides. The pink dragonfly fabric is a little bit of both, as I was using as many scraps as possible.

As strange as it seems, it doesn't bother me to mix and match types of cuts. A little starch substitute helps to control them. And after all, I'm just trying to make the best quilt possible and often that means bending the rules a little. The more quilts you make, the more confident you become.

With those decisions made, cut 36 dark triangles, 16 light triangles and 16 medium triangles and pin them in place on your work wall. The medium and light triangles are interchangeable. On this quilt the dark center triangles are surrounded by the medium check.

On the variation quilt the dark center is flanked by the light valued triangles. Try it both ways and go with your favorite.

Now is a good time to audition your sashing and border possibilities. In both of these quilts, I've repeated the medallion fabric for the borders. The sashing is a solid color and the corner block repeats one of the triangle prints.

But before we cut these pieces, let's put together the body of your quilt. First we must assemble all the blocks starting with the top row. As you take them off the wall, stack them in pairs so they are easy to keep track of. Stitch these pairs together in a continuous string. Cut them apart and press each seam to set it. Then open the block and press all seams toward the dark fabric. Pin the blocks back up and repeat until all the two piece blocks are finished.

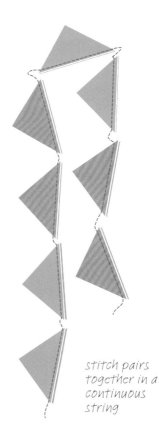

stitch pairs together in a continuous string

medallion block

Sew together the medallion block.

Next we will sew the blocks into rows. On the first row press the seams toward the dark fabrics. On the second row press the seams toward the lighter fabrics. Keep alternating the directions of the seams by row. This will enable them to nest nicely together.

Now we can join the rows together. Pin the edges to keep the corners fitting snugly and stitch row 1 to row 2. Repeat for each row, even though you only have short rows in the middle. Press all these seams open.

Sew the middle rows to the center medallion. Press the seams to nest with the neighboring rows. Now we have three sections to pin and sew together. Press these seams open.

Cut five selvedge to selvedge strips 2" wide for a 1½" finished sashing. Piece these strips together to make two that are 42½" long and two that are 45½".

Stitch the two shorter strips to opposite sides of the quilt and press seams toward the sashing. Attach the remaining strips to the other sides and press as before.

Fussy-cut five or six identical 7½" strips for the border (7" finished) and piece them together so the pattern is continuous and the joins are invisible (see page 53).

Decide how you'd like to center the fabric's design on the borders. Then cut four of these identical border sections.

Cut four 7½" corner squares. Pin and stitch borders onto opposite sides and press the seams toward the borders. Sew a corner square to the ends of the last two border strips and press seams toward the borders, again. Nest the corners and attach the final borders and press seams open.

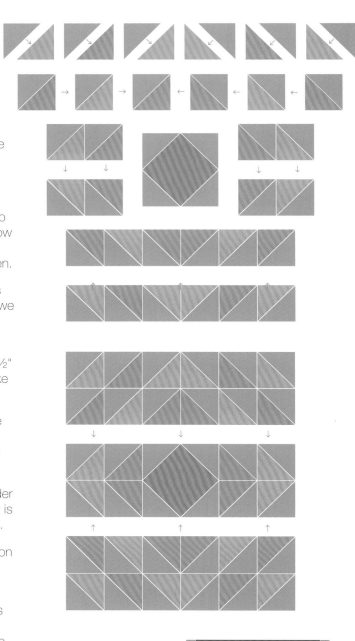

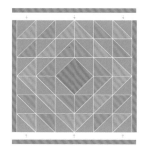

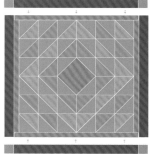

Jack's Journey

Jack's Journey is a wonderful example of transparency in a quilt. Look at the light, medium and dark triangles. The light and dark fabrics have nothing in common, but the medium fabric combines colors from those disparate triangles and blends them all perfectly. The corner blocks have been divided diagonally to carry through the movement of the waves.

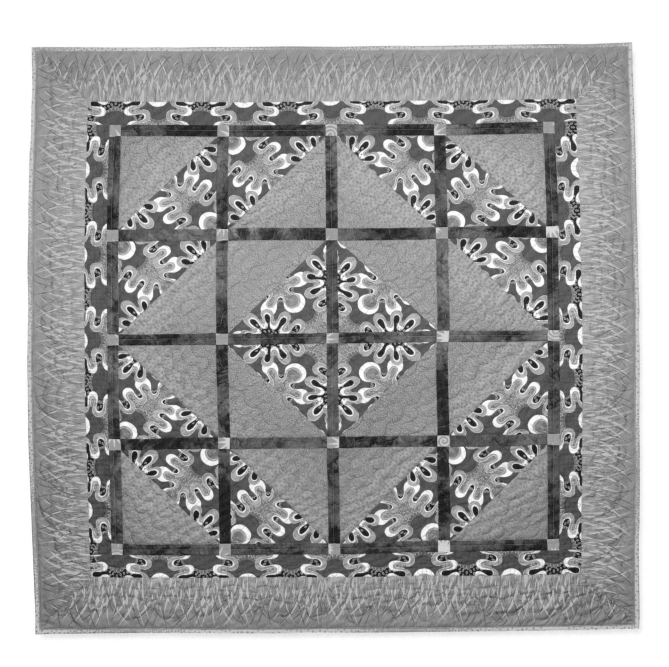

Rowdy Barn Raising

This energetic variation features fewer blocks in a larger scale. This adjustment was made to take advantage of the large symmetrical print. This print is fussy cut, so the triangles were all cut individually. The blue grid of sashing ties the fabrics together. The bright green setting squares echo the grassy green border. Truly a rowdy barn raising party!

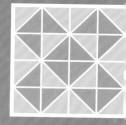

Mirrored Triangles

In this recipe we are using half-square triangles again, but the blocks are much larger because the print is bigger. We are also using two colorways of the same fabric. Each block has identical fussy-cut triangles in both colorways, so one half is a mirror image of the other, but in a different color.

This technique won't work with all fabrics because some colorways are radically different from each other. But in this *Magic Forest* fabric, the two colorways have some of the same colors. Both fabrics have yellow and green in common, so they play together nicely. But the red and purple almost clash and this creates excitement.

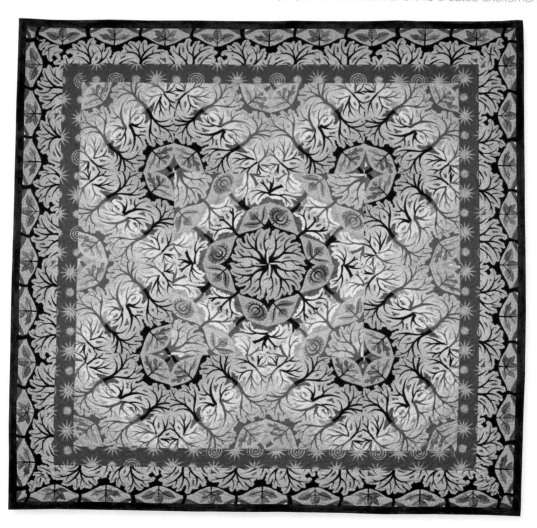

Choose a fabric design with an easy to see symmetrical horizontal repeat. The two colorways of this design should share some common colors.

The sashing shares a similar color to the triangles it touches and echoes the red square in the middle. The border simply reuses the purple fabrics and ties the whole piece together. The purple binding blends with the border and provides a gentle finish for all the activity in the middle.

After the fabric is chosen, decide on the size of your block. As always, this depends on the scale of the print.

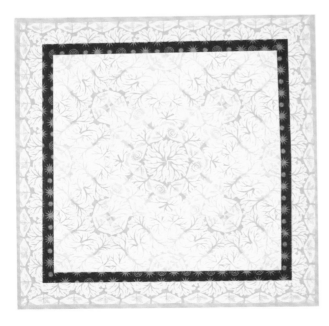

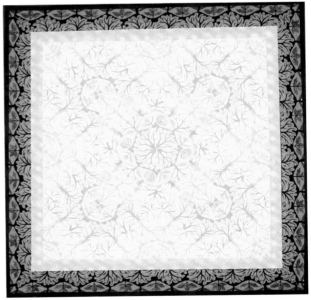

To make this quilt, we will again cut strips of fabric (like the Barn Raising Quilt) and sew them in alternating mirrored rows. But this time, each row must be the same fussy cut over and over in both colorways.

Our sample quilt is made of 12" blocks, so our template is a 12½" square. As before, make your 12½" template and draw a line diagonally from corner to corner. To determine the width of your strips measure the height of the triangle from the center of the block and add an inch. This allows for the space that will be taken up with seam allowances and leave a little leeway for adjustments. For your 12½" template the triangle height is about 9", so I would cut my strips 10" wide. Each 10" strip must be the identical cut from both colors of fabric.

The number of blocks you can cut will vary according to the fabric's horizontal repeat. To determine the numbers of strips you will need, cut one strip from both colorways and sew them together so the designs mirror one another. Notice that the trees in this fabric are not perfectly symmetrical, but lean slightly one way. I have chosen to match up the tree trunks as best as possible.

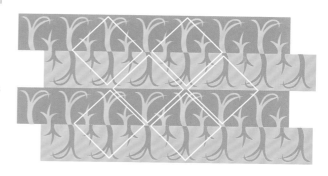

Often the designs are not centered perfectly between selvedges and so matching the print does not guarantee that you can use the whole width of the fabric. In every other row the blocks will be the same, one row the tops of trees and the next row the bottoms.

In our sample quilt, there are two sets of blocks, four in the center that have trees at the tip of each triangle and 12 surrounding blocks that have leaves at the top of each triangle. But the trick is to audition several possible arrangements and see which one works best.

Once that is decided, consider the sashing. Here the sashing is 2½" finished. This is a little wider than usual because it provides us with a rest from all the inner energy.

The border is 5" wide and the fussy cut strips are pieced together in an uninterrupted pattern. The corners are mitered to keep the eyes flowing smoothly around the quilt.

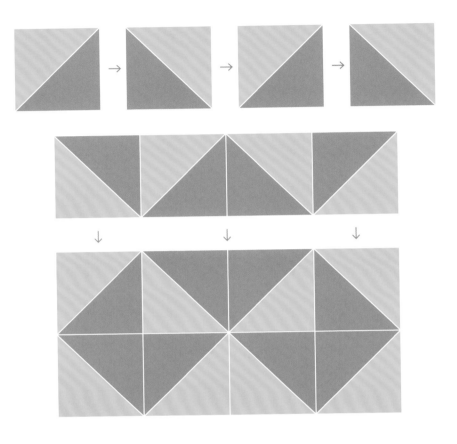

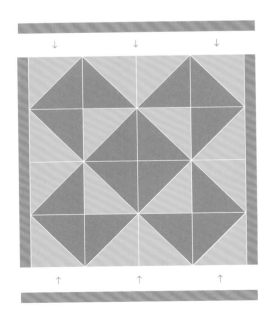

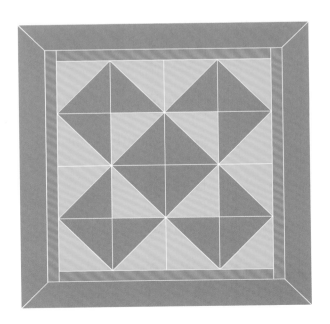

Bouquet Reflections

Bouquet Reflections also uses three colorways of a single fabric design. But in this case, there are four triangles (quarter-square triangles) in each block. The more you look, the more you notice. Cropping here, too, creates some wonderful effects as the patterns interact.

Primrose Variation

This is one of my all-time favorite quilts made with my Free Spirit fabrics. So many surprising effects happened when putting these mirror-imaged blocks together.

If you look carefully, you will see there are actually three different colorways of a single design cut into half-square triangles: one with a yellow background, one with blue and one with black. The blocks are 12" square and arranged on point.

The surface of this beautiful quilt looks so complex and sophisticated, yet the piecing is basic. The fabric is doing all the work here. The cropping is also an important factor. Cutting off the tips of the leaves allowed the leaves to arch and blend together, giving this quilt an accidental reminiscence of Louis Sullivan's elegant architectural ornamentation.

I usually begin with at least one and half yards of three different fabrics. If needed other fabrics can be added eventually, but three symmetrical prints that share similar colors in varying amounts is a good place to start.

When you study our sample quilt, you will notice that it is made of interlacing rows of triangles. One row has four whole triangles and the next has three whole and two half-triangles.

The fun part of making this quilt is trying all the configurations, so I like to begin by cutting a strip of each fabric that is slightly wider than my template (treated with starch substitute) and fussy cutting as many whole triangles that feature the symmetrical designs. Don't worry about the half triangles at this

point, but set aside your scraps to use later.

After you have done this for all three fabrics you will have a nice collection of triangles to play with. Pin them on your work wall with identical cuts in the same horizontal row. This is the time to get out your digital camera and record your arrangement. Now switch the rows around until they are playing nicely together. Give yourself some rules to help organize the shapes. For example, arrange them from light to dark rows. Or dark in the middle and light rows at the edges. How about alternating rows by color? Can you make the edges of the triangles blend together?

This is not a speedy process, because there are so many possibilities.

These compositions involve lots of manipulation and contemplation. Just enjoy the journey. Don't forget to try some of the alternative layouts, too. Add a new fabric if needed.

Once you have a nice composition, you can add the half triangles to complete the rows. Be sure you have added the extra seam allowance to your half-triangle template.

Now it is time to audition sashing and border fabrics. There is so much activity in the center of the quilt that a simple sashing fabric is best. The sashing will contain and concentrate the energy. The border is the icing on the cake. It must relate to the colors and textures within the quilt, but also finalize the composition.

Most of the effort for making this quilt is in the designing but the construction of this quilt is very simple. As before, we will work a row at a time beginning at the top. When piecing the triangles together, lay right sides together and allow the corners to slightly peak out the ends for the quarter-inch seam allowance.

Begin by piecing pairs. Press the seams open for each pair. Then sew the pairs to each other and press as before. Repeat for each row. Then pin row one to row two. Line up all points and pin them together. Pay attention to these joins as you stitch through them. Press the seam open and continue down through the rows.

When the body of the quilt is finished, cut two sashing strips the length of your quilt top and stitch them to opposite sides. Cut two more sashing strips the length of the remaining sides and attach. Press these seams toward the sashing. The border fabric on our sample quilt has mitered corners, see page 25 for directions.

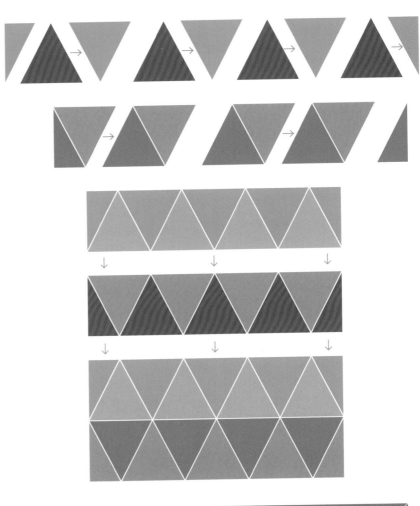

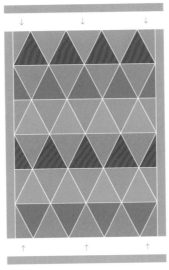

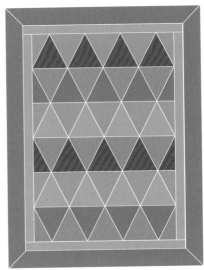

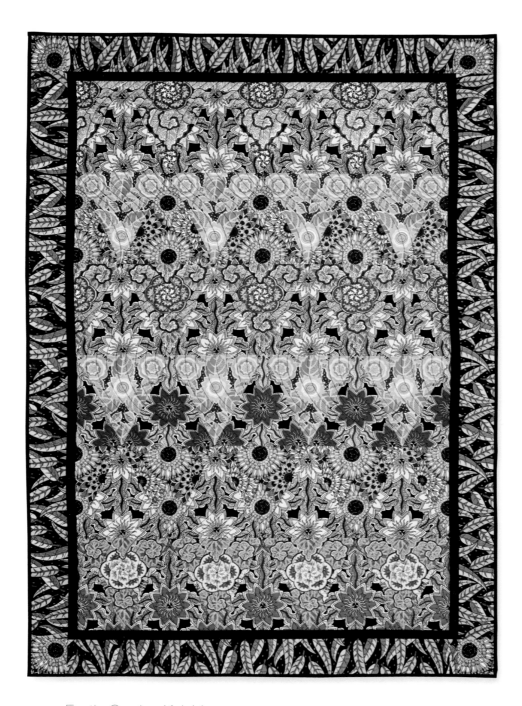

Exotic Garden Kaleidoscope

Our variation quilt is exactly the same pattern as our recipe quilt. The only differences are the fabrics and the corner blocks in the border. I think these quilts show the exciting potential of the Thousand Mountains pattern. One of my favorites!

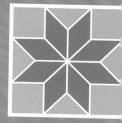

LeMoyne Star

I have had stunning results with the LeMoyne Star and its big sister, the Broken Star. The body of this quilt is made with only three large, simple shapes—a 45° diamond, an 8½" square (9" template) and its half-square triangle. The star in the center is made of eight fussy-cut diamonds and the square and half square fill the space around the star.

Depending on your fabric choices, this quilt can be very stark and simple or extremely opulent. The star can be easy to see or next to impossible to spot, as in all of our samples. I have a hard time being subtle when designing for the LeMoyne and Broken Stars. The combination of radiating shapes mixed with symmetrical fabric is pretty intoxicating.

After studying the recipe quilt, you may realize that it is constructed with just two colorways of the same fabric design, so it was necessary to add a thin black sashing to separate these very active elements.

Use your folding mirrors to audition symmetrical fabrics for the center star of eight identical fussy-cut diamonds. Once you have settled on a fabric, test different sections for the most interesting effects. The surrounding square and half-square both share the same fabric. These pieces are also symmetrical fussy cuts, so the design radiates in a circle around the star. I wait to audition the border fabric until after the center of the quilt has been made.

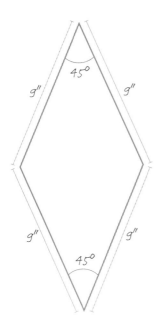

Piecing this quilt is not hard, but you do need to take care when cutting your shapes so they will fit together nicely. For this reason I recommend that you wash, spritz with starch substitute and iron your fabric to preshrink and stabilize it before cutting. If this is not possible, at least spritz the fabric with starch substitute and iron it well before cutting. This is because the fabric shapes can shrink if spritzed and pressed after they are cut. These shapes need to be of a consistent size for accurate assembly.

Since accuracy is important when making this pattern, it is best to use a perfectly engineered tool for cutting the diamonds. I have a favorite commercial template for the LeMoyne and Broken Stars, Jan Krentz's Fussy Cutter 45° Diamond Ruler. This large diamond (15½" long and 6½" wide finished) is the perfect size to make a dramatic statement. I supplement this ruler with my homemade 8½" finished square (9" template) and an 8½" half-square triangle template. I store them as a set in a large plastic bag for easy access.

After ironing, mark your template to help line up the selected motif for fussy cutting the diamonds. Then carefully cut eight identical symmetrical diamonds. Since all the diamonds are bias cut, handle these shapes gently and pin them to your work wall, beginning with the top two diamonds

Take a photo of the star.

Now flip the diamonds the other direction just to see what happens. How does this change the design? Which arrangement looks better? Sometimes the unplanned results are better than the original idea.

At this point you can fussy cut the four squares and four half-square triangles, both from the same motif.

Again mark the templates, if necessary, to line up the same portion of the print for each cut. These shapes may need to be cut on the bias, depending on the design of the fabric. Pin these to your work wall. How do they look?

Take their picture and flip the squares to see how the quilt top changes. If this is better, you will need to re-cut the half square triangles accordingly. With all these decisions made, we can now assemble the body of the quilt.

Because an accurate seam allowance is essential for the pieces to fit together properly, use your quarter-inch sewing machine foot or adjust the needle position to stitch a scant quarter-inch seam.

The first unit we will put together is called a "baby's block", because it looks like a child's building block in perspective. It consists of two diamonds and a square.

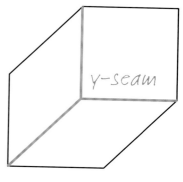

A baby's block has set-in seams, which is something we haven't encountered before in this book. A set-in seam is also called a "Y" seam, because the square (and half square) is set-in the opening between two diamonds.

So these pieces need to be sewn a little differently.

First use your ruler and pencil to lightly mark an accurate quarter-inch seam allowance on the back corners of all your shapes.

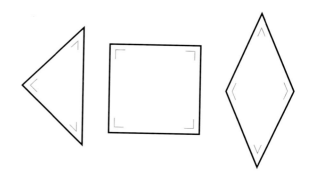

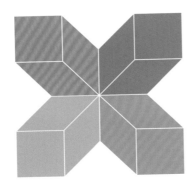

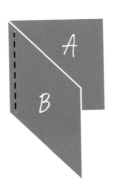

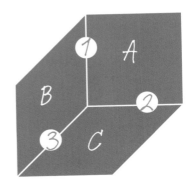

Look at your final photograph and you will see four baby's blocks – one in each corner.

We will begin by stitching each individual block unit first. With right sides together, pin square A to diamond B along seam 1. Put the pins through the quarter-inch marks to align the pieces.

Sew between the quarter-inch marks, backstitching at the beginning and end.

Do not press your seams until the whole body is pieced together. Lay diamond C over square A and pin and stitch seam 2 just as before. Now pin seam three and stitch. Repeat this process for each corner block.

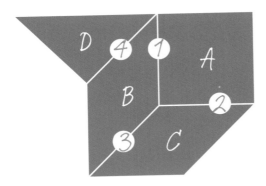

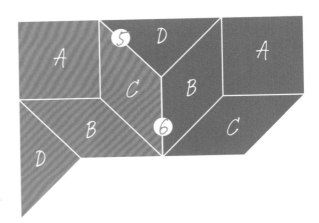

Next we will attach a half-square triangle to each baby's block unit. Lay shape D over shape B and pin seam 4. Stitch between marks as always. Repeat for each baby's block.

Now we can attach two corner units together.

Pin seam 5 and stitch and pin and stitch seam 6.

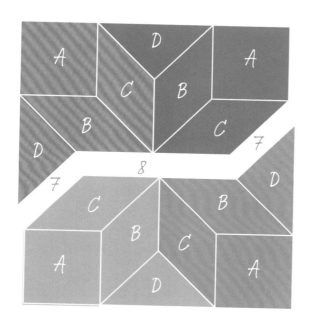

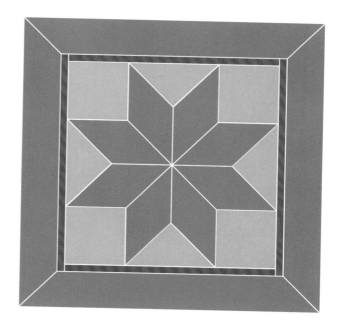

Repeat for the other half of the units. Now you have two matching halves.

Pin and stitch seam 7 on both ends. Pin and machine baste seam 8. Check that both centers line up. Then sew it together permanently.

Your star is complete and ready for pressing. Press the seams systematically in the same directions. Press the star seams in the same direction to form a pinwheel in the center. Press the seams on the outer edges of the diamonds toward the squares or triangles. This takes a little patience, but is worth your time to press it neatly.

Our recipe quilt needed a row of sashing between the body of the quilt and the border as a respite from all the opulent pattern.

Cut two 1½" wide sashing strips that are the length of your quilt top—29½" if using Jan's diamond template. Then attach them to opposite sides. Press seams toward the sashing. Cut two more strips that are 32" or the length of the remaining sides. Stitch them down and press as before.

The border width for this quilt measures slightly less than the height of the triangle so approximately 5½" finished, cut six or more 6" border strips, depending how the design is positioned. These strips may need to be pieced together to allow a continuous (uninterrupted) print that can be centered on each side. Make four 46" lengths; since the corners are mitered we need to make them a little longer than the final measurement of the quilt. Pin and stitch each side starting and stopping ¼" from both ends. Follow the mitering directions on page 25 to complete.

Lacy Star

In the Lacy Star variation, the solid shapes lose their definition, seams disappear and motifs dissolve into one another. This happens because both the diamond and the surrounding squares and triangles all have a black background. This time there is not any sashing to separate the border and the body of the quilt. Instead the repeating arches of pink bleeding hearts create a pleasant frame which echoes the pink in the center of the quilt. The same fabric is used for the star and the border. The mitered corners are a handsome finishing touch.

Bleeding Heart Star

You may recognize some familiar fabric in this variation. Yes, those are the same bleeding hearts and irises as in the Lacy Star, except in this quilt they are cut as the squares and triangles. The extra exuberance of this fabric combination again required the restful sashing to separate all the colorful activity. And, as in each of these LeMoyne quilts, the star and the border share the same fabric.

Isn't it amazing that all of these quilts are made from the same pattern? Proof of the power in large symmetrical prints. Just let the fabric do the work.

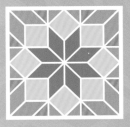

Broken Star

The Broken Star is just an expanded version of the LeMoyne Star. Look at the illustration and you will see the LeMoyne design in the middle.

We will be using the same templates from the last chapter except we will be cutting more pieces from each one.

For our recipe quilt, *Emerald Jack Star*, we are using only four fabrics, including the solid border. The patterned fabrics are not symmetrical this time, but they are still fussy-cut and arranged to create a definite pattern.

I always design these quilts from the center out. Each successive row is reacting to its predecessors. There is a lot of arranging and rearranging before the pieces find their proper place. So audition your star fabrics first. The *Jack-in-the-Pulpit* fabric here had flowers going one direction in one row and the other direction in the next. It would be more efficient (less wasteful) to use them as mirror image cuts, so that is how I proceeded. They still join together in a delightfully kaleidoscopic way.

The next layer out is the wreath of squares, which I filled with green fronds that are fussy-cut to radiate from the middle of the quilt and reveal the same amount of "curl" at top and bottom. They are also arranged in alternating light and dark green squares.

Stepping outward again we have a wreath of diamonds. I chose to repeat the same cuts of the flower pattern as before. These diamond pairs mirror one another and are separated by a purple frond fabric. The purple fronds are also cut so their linear design radiates from the center.

Next we have another ring of green fronds, but this time they are cut and placed to mirror its partner. They are not the same, really, but they all contain the same elements in the same proportions to give the illusion of regularity.

Radiating purple blocks in the corner create bookends to contain the star; the blue border contains and coordinates with all the action in the middle.

What to cut?

Cut 4 squares on point of purple frond

Cut 8 purple frond diamonds

Cut 8 squares on point of green frond

Cut 8 regular squares green frond

Cut 8 half squares triangles green frond

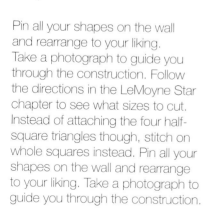

Cut 16 left flowers

Cut 16 right flowers

Pin all your shapes on the wall and rearrange to your liking. Take a photograph to guide you through the construction. Follow the directions in the LeMoyne Star chapter to see what sizes to cut. Instead of attaching the four half-square triangles though, stitch on whole squares instead. Pin all your shapes on the wall and rearrange to your liking. Take a photograph to guide you through the construction.

Look at the diagram and stitch together the outer groups as shown; continue making the set-in squares and triangles as before.

When all these units are complete,

attach them to the central unit one at a time, working around the top until they are all sewn together. Press the central star seams in the same direction and press the other star seams toward the squares. Press the outer diamond seams toward the squares and half-squares. Press the outermost block seams toward the outer block.

The border is made by cutting 3¼" strips and piecing them together. Cut two border strips the length of your quilt (58" with Jan's Diamond Ruler) and attach to opposite sides of the quilt. Cut two more 64" strips for the final two sides.

Spider Web Kaleidoscope

This mysterious quilt is one of my all-time favorites. It is made with four fabrics from the *Prairie Gothic* line. All the fabrics have a black background except the *Queen Anne's Lace* at the very edges, but it has a very dark blue which is almost as dark. These symmetrical fabric designs also have an interweaving variety of textures and scales. It is always interesting to look at.

Solar Star

This quilt is designed with only three fabrics. The turquoise and yellow grass shoots sunshine all through this quilt. Even the glowing border is made with the grass fabric. I am always amazed at the variety of attitudes this pattern can create.

Cosmic Star

This broken star variation is quite lively. It is made of three fabrics in the same colors, but in different proportions. As the design radiates from the center, circles of distinct color appear, but each layer of color blends subtly into its neighbor. The blue border speaks to the blues that are sprinkled throughout the quilt and helps to tie this spirited composition together.

Grandmother's Flower Garden

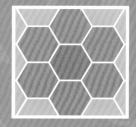

This recipe rescales a traditional quilt design into the modern age. Instead of the tiny hexagons of the past, this Grandmother's Flower Garden makes a commanding statement with oversized five inch hexagons. Plus the vertical format adds to the drama as do the contrasting colors.

The large hexagon is well-suited for featuring fussy-cut fabrics with symmetrical prints. When the same cuts are grouped together, they form a kaleidoscopic wreath. Each wreath is a different cut from the same fabric giving each one an individual personality.

The red in the center anchors each wreath and also holds them visually together. The bright orange hexagons set off the darker totem of wreaths.

This is the only hand sewn recipe in this book, so it is a good project to pick up and work on when you have a free minute or two.

Begin with a main wreath fabric that has an obvious symmetrical print. Consider the areas you would like to fussy cut. Choose a solid color for the wreath's center. It should be a color that each wreath has in common. This is the same criterion for the surrounding shapes, but they should be lighter and brighter. One of the bright fabrics should be a symmetrical print and the other a solid color included in the bright print.

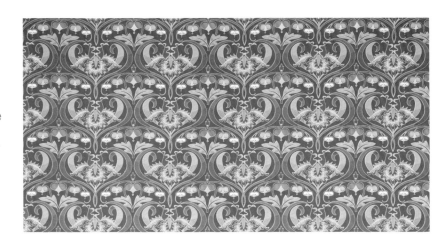

Constructing the quilt

Of course you can make your own hexagon templates for this quilt, but I recommend that you use a commercial template because they are precisely engineered and will guarantee that your pieces fit together nicely.

We will be using a new tool in this recipe, freezer paper. It is sold in the paper products section of your grocery store and comes in a roll like waxed paper. The paper has a shiny coating on one side which temporarily adheres to fabric when ironed. It also makes a nice crisp edge for folding fabric against so it is a material used for traditional hand appliqué.

Trace 34 whole hexagons (A), 24 half hexagons (B) and 4 half hexagons (C) onto the dull side of your freezer paper.

Use a craft knife and ruler to cut the shapes apart. The more exact you cut, the better your pieces will fit together.

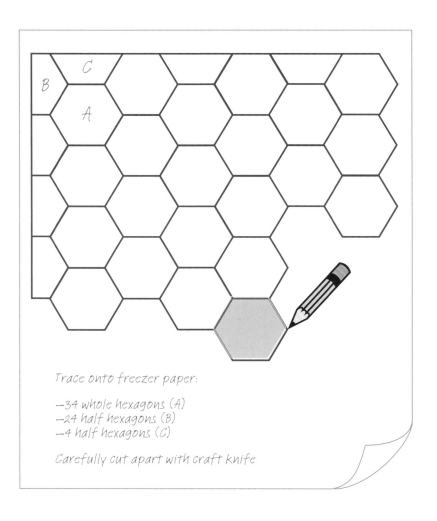

Trace onto freezer paper:

—34 whole hexagons (A)
—24 half hexagons (B)
—4 half hexagons (C)

Carefully cut apart with craft knife

Fuse four sets of six hexagons on the back of your wreath fabrics. Then freehand cut a generous ¼" seam allowance around each shape. Place a hexagon face down on your ironing surface and paint the seam allowance on one straight side with starch substitute. Then fold and press the allowance snugly over the edge of the paper. Continue around the hexagon, one side at a time, until all the seams are pressed flat. Repeat this process for all the wreath hexagons.

Fuse four whole hexagons for the wreath centers. Cut, paint, fold and press as before.

Fuse six whole hexagons, eight half hexagons (B) and four half hexagons (C) of the bright symmetrical print. Cut, paint, fold and press.

Fuse 16 half hexagons (B) to the solid bright fabric and treat as all the others.

If you will be transporting this handwork project from place to place, I recommend that you hand baste the seam allowances in place. But if the pieces are just sitting in your sewing box between stitching sessions, basting may not be necessary.

When all the shapes are pressed and the edges are turned, pin them to your work wall and arrange them to your liking. Take a photograph of the top and print it as a sewing reference guide.

Each individual wreath will be assembled first. Place a center hexagon and a wreath hexagon with their faces together. Pin them so the edges meet.

Use a new knotted thread for each side, hiding the beginning knot under the seam.

Whipstitch (with tiny stitches) two straight edges together catching only the top 2-4 threads. Refer to your photograph to be sure you are stitching the correct edges together. When you finish a side, make a French knot and hide the end under the folded edge and clip. Sewing each edge with an individual thread will make the quilt top more stable and easier to repair later, if necessary. Continue around until the wreath is complete.

As your quilt top grows, you will find it necessary to fold sections for easier sewing access.

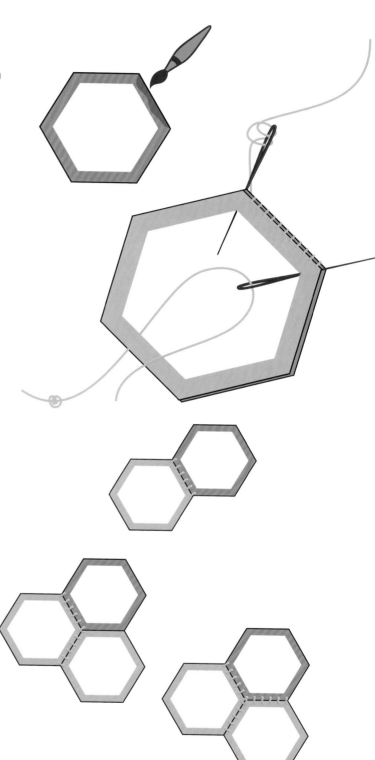

When all the wreaths are stitched, refer to your photograph and begin attaching the pieces around each wreath until the top is all sewn together. Press it flat so all the seams are in place. If your seam allowances were basted, now is the time to take the basting thread out. Then carefully remove the paper backing. Square up the ends and sides with a ruler.

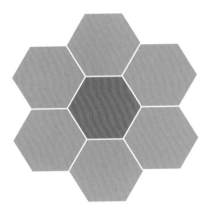

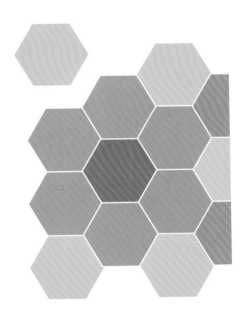

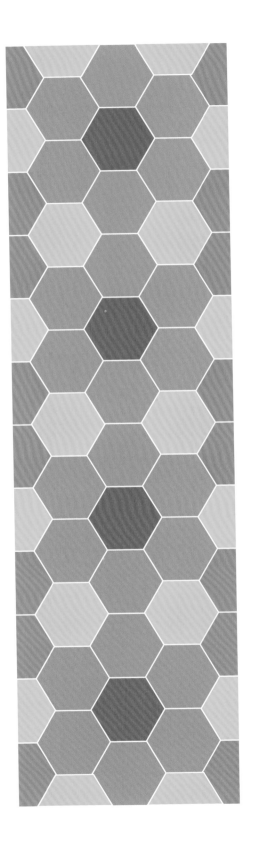

Dragonfly Garland

This Grandmother's Flower Garden variation is made from the exact same pattern as the original, yet it has a very different flavor. Of course, it is the choice of fabrics that makes the difference.

It varies, too, because the dragonfly hexagons are all the same fussy cut, so all the pink circlets are the same. The sprinkle of yellow dots in the secondary units ties them to the color in the center and their blue background makes a transition to the blue dotted fabric around the edge. The striped binding brings the composition to a gentle but witty finish.

I am very excited about the possibilities of this pattern. I think these modern interpretations are very sophisticated compared to the little pastel variations of the past.

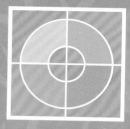
The Fan pattern is a favorite for graphic interplay between light and dark fabrics. I make my fan blocks as appliqués, but they can be made by piecing as well. For this recipe the block is 12" finished (12½" template) and cut from three colorways of the same spotted fabric. The fans are also made from two colorations of the same print. The light fans are placed over the darker backgrounds and the dark fans are paired with the light squares. The 2" border (cut 2½" strips) is made from another variation of the dotted fabric.

Audition fabrics for the fans. Choose a large print in both light and dark versions. These fabrics should play together nicely, not clash. Choose a simple print or solid fabric in several coordinating colors for the background and border.

Make the fan template. First draw a 12" square, then draw a ¼" seam allowance on all sides. Place your compass point in the bottom corner of the 12" square and draw a circle segment 3½" from the point. Then make another segment ¼" from the bottom 12" mark.

Trace four fan shapes (including seam allowance on the straight edges only) onto the nonstick side of your iron-on interfacing and cut them out loosely. Iron-on interfacing is an interfacing with adhesive on one side. It is used as a stabilizer and is ironed to the back of the fabric. Fuse these fans to the back of your fan fabrics, two dark and two light. If the print is symmetrical, center the design. Now cut the fans out exactly on the drawn lines. Cut four 12½" background squares, two light and two dark. Lay the dark fans on the light squares and vice versa. Line up the edges and pin them in place. Straight stitch close to the curved edges (¹⁄₁₆"). Then finish the curved edges with an open satin stitch (approximate width 4.0 and length 0.6). Cut away the extra fabric of the background square from behind the fans.

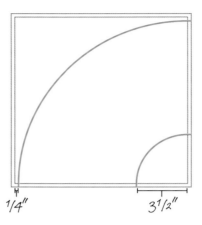

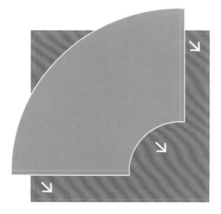

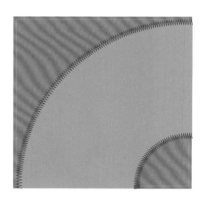

Satin stitch, enlarged view:

good spacing

too tight

Back of block:

cut away background fabric behind the fan

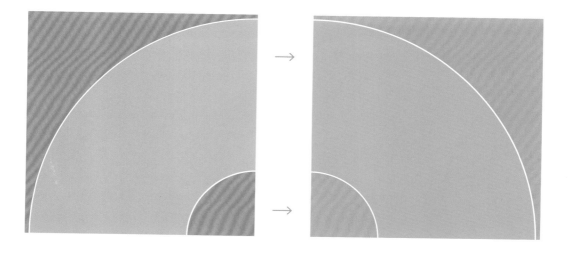

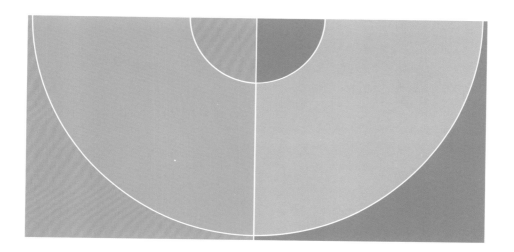

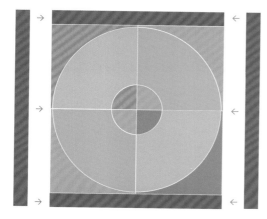

Just as in the previous recipes, we will piece these blocks by rows.

Press the seams toward the darker fabric. Then sew the rows to each other and press the seam open.

Cut two 2½" border strips the length of your quilt top (24½") and attach them to opposite sides. Press the seams toward the borders. Cut two more border strips (29") and attach to the remaining sides.

Hugs and Kisses

The *Hugs and Kisses* quilt is made very much the same as the recipe quilt, except the fans are thinner and their curved edges are turned and topstitched, as opposed to raw edge and finished with satin stitch. The blocks are the same size but there are more of them, making a stunningly stark quilt with major graphic impact.

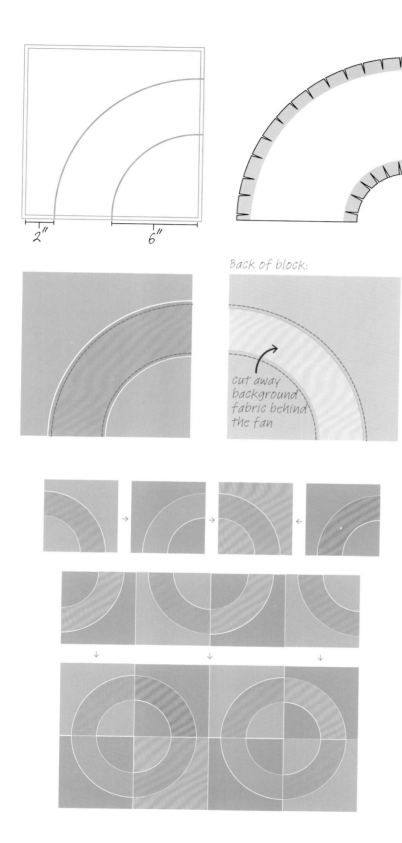

2"   6"

Back of block:

cut away background fabric behind the fan

To make the fan templates, draw a 12" square and its ¼" seam allowance as before. This time draw a circle segment 6" from the compass point and another 2" from the opposite corner.

Trace the 16 arcs, including the seam allowances at the straight ends, onto the nonstick side of your iron-on interfacing and cut them out exactly. Fuse them to the back of your print fabric and cut around each leaving approximately ¼" around the curved edges. Clip the extra fabric for turning.

Finger press the tabs to the back and then press them again with a steam iron so the tabs are folded smooth, flat and tight against the interfacing edges. There are three colors of background blocks. Cut six 12½" green squares, eight dark blue and two light pink. Pin the blocks to your wall in a checkerboard pattern. Now pin the fans on top; light fans on dark backgrounds and vice versa.

Play with this arrangement until you are happy with the composition. Using your open-toed embroidery foot, topstitch (12 weight thread) each fan onto the appropriate background, $^1/_{16}$" from the curved edges. Cut the extra background fabric from behind each fan. Assemble as usual; first sew the blocks into rows and then sew the rows to each other. The border is also attached as usual.

Big-Hearted Quilt

This quilt combines appliqué and piecing for a folk art feeling. The large hearts, flowers and corner sprigs are all appliquéd to background blocks and then the blocks are sewn together.

This is also a high contrast quilt. In this case, the purple and lime green are nearly opposites on the color wheel, but they are also acting as a light and a dark. Dark hearts on a light ground and light hearts on a dark background create a checkerboard pattern in the center of the quilt. Each heart is also outlined with black zigzags to add more definition and some extra vigor.

The large half-square triangles are fussy cut to take advantage of the fabric's design. The white and purple sashing adds a bit of sparkle and echoes the white appliquéd flowers as do the pink setting blocks. The coordinated border adds to the atmosphere of the quilt by repeating the colors from the center. The final sashing also acts as an extra border. It holds the composition together.

All these fabrics come from the same colorway of a single collection, so they are especially calibrated to work together. This is true for most of the quilts in this book, because they were made to feature the current line of that season. But please remember that there are many designer fabrics that play nicely with each other. Look in your stash and make combinations by color and design and I'm sure you will find some perfect fabrics to make your own Big-Hearted Quilt.

Find two contrasting tone on tone (or simple prints) fabrics for your hearts. And then look for a coordinating print with the same colors for the large half-square triangles. The quarter-square triangles (under the sprigs) are a very simple coordinating print. Take a cue from the printed fabric for the color of the heart's zig zag border and the daisy appliqué.

I wait to audition sashing and borders until I have the entire panel of the quilt cut and pinned to my work wall.

You will need a new tool to make this quilt: fusible web. Fusible web is a double-sided adhesive web that is protected by paper on one side and sticks to your fabric with a hot dry iron.

The whole blocks in the center of this quilt are 17½" finished. This means that the heart and daisy appliqué must fit inside this block when it is set on point.

Enlarge all 300%

To make your appliqués, enlarge the templates 300% or until the smooth heart is 15" across. This can be done at your local print shop. Trace 5 zigzag hearts, 5 flower centers and 4 leafy spirals onto the protective paper side of your fusible web. Trace 5 smooth hearts and 5 flowers (whole, without center circle) onto the non-sticky side of your fusible interfacing. Cut out shapes just beyond the traced lines.

Fuse the zigzag hearts to the wrong side of the zigzag fabric. Fuse the flower centers to the wrong side of the appropriate fabric. Fuse the leafy spirals to the wrong side of its fabric. Cut out the shapes neatly on the traced lines.

Fuse 4 smooth hearts to the wrong side of your light fabric. Fuse 1 heart to the wrong side of your dark fabric. Fuse your flowers to your daisy fabric. Cut the shapes out neatly on the traced lines.

Take the protective paper off the flower center and fuse it onto the flower. Using a matching thread, finish or capture the raw edges around the circle with a satin stitch. When the circuit is finished, pull all threads to the back side, tie them in a knot and clip.

To make the appliquéd blocks, cut out four 18" dark (17 ½" finished) squares and one of the light fabric. Strip the protective paper from the zigzag hearts. Center a flower and a zigzag heart on all five blocks. Pin the flowers in position. Fuse the zigzag hearts into place.

With matching thread, straight stitch the flower very close to its edge and then finish the edge with a zigzag stitch. Using matching thread, satin stitch around the zigzag hearts. Pull threads to the back, tie and clip.

Center the smooth hearts over the zigzag hearts. Dark hearts on the light blocks and the light heart on the dark block. Pin and straight stitch around the extreme edge and finish with a matching satin stitch. Carefully cut away the fabric from behind the smooth hearts.

Cut four 17½" (finished size) half-square triangles from the print fabric, being sure to fussy cut the same portion of the design for each triangle.

Now cut four quarter-square triangles for each corner from a simple coordinated print. Center and fuse the sprigs to the triangle and finish with a matching satin stitch.

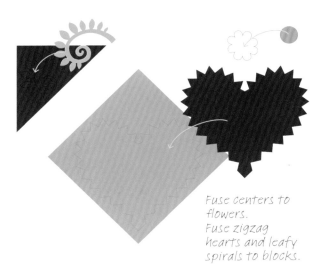

*Fuse centers to flowers.
Fuse zigzag hearts and leafy spirals to blocks.*

Stitch whole flowers and smooth hearts to blocks. Trim away fabric behind flower and heart.

Finish edges with a satin stitch

Sew the blocks in diagonal rows and press the seams toward the dark fabric. Sew the rows together and press seams open.

Audition fabric for your sashing, setting squares and border. When this decision has been made, cut five 2¼" selvedge to selvedge strips of sashing fabric. Cut eight 2¼" squares from the setting square fabric.

Piece sashing strips end to end and cut into four 50" lengths. Attach two strips to opposite sides and press seam toward the sashing. Sew a pink square to both ends of the two remaining strips. Press seams toward the sashing. Attach the strips to the other two sides.

Fussy cut six 6½" selvedge to selvedge strips from the border fabric. Piece the rows together so the design is uninterrupted. Cut into two 53½" strips and attach to opposite sides. Press seams toward the border.

Cut two 65½" border strips and sew to the other two sides. Press seams toward the border.

Cut six more 2¼" sashing strips. Piece them end to end and cut into 65½" lengths. Stitch a strip to opposite sides and press seams toward the border.

Add the remaining setting squares to the ends of the last two strips. Press seams toward the corner and attach to opposite edges.

Press seams open.

Folk Art Hearts

This vibrant variation of the Big-Hearted Quilt was made with fabrics from the *Hothouse Garden* collection. The heart blocks are the same size but the main difference is the motif which is partnered with the heart. For Folk Art Hearts, I fussy cut a flame-like appliqué to slip behind the heart motif. The purple dotted zigzags behind the hearts blend with the background of the flame. The half-square triangles are also pieced–note the mitered corners.

This quilt is perfect for large prints, symmetrical or not. The pattern is laid out in a checkerboard of 12" finished dark and light blocks. The nine light blocks contain an appliquéd butterfly. The dark blocks in the middle of the quilt are made in two different fabrics. The half-square triangles at top and bottom are all cut from the same fabric.

The border fabric is also dark and blends nicely into the half-square triangles around the edges.

All the fabrics in this quilt are from the same collection, so there is a natural camaraderie between them. But this is a great pattern for mixing and matching from your stash. For example, each butterfly could be made with a different yellow fabric. Novelty fabrics could be fun, too.

There are two styles of butterflies, a round butterfly and a spiky one. They are all made with two pieces of fabric, a dark silhouette underneath and a colorful print on top.

Choose a simple light print for the block behind the butterflies. You want the butterflies to be easy to see. Next audition the dark fabrics. They should all play together nicely. Which dark fabric would be best for the triangles at the top and bottom?

Each butterfly is different, so you need a stack of 9 coordinating fabrics. I chose black for the silhouette because there was lots of black in my dark fabrics and black would set off the bright colors nicely.

Begin by making the blocks. Cut nine 12½" light blocks.

There are two whole and two pieced dark blocks in the center of the quilt. The pieced blocks are made of fussy cut mirror-imaged squares that are 6" finished (6 ½" template).

So cut the two whole blocks so the print is centered. Then fussy cut two sets of four mirrored squares. Piece the squares together.

The half-square triangles on the sides are whole pieces from the same fabrics. Cut these out and pin all your shapes to your work wall.

Next we will cut the half and quarter-square triangles for the top and bottom rows from your last dark fabric. Notice however, that the fabric faces the same direction, but the triangles change direction, so pay attention when cutting them. Pin them to your wall.

Now for the appliquéd butterflies. You will need fusible web and iron-on interfacing. Enlarge the butterfly patterns 300% or until the butterflies fit in the 12" block.

Trace the outer line for the background silhouette shape and the inner line for the colorful top layer.

Trace five spiky and four round butterfly silhouettes (outer line) onto the protective paper side of your fusible web. Cut these roughly outside the line and fuse them to the back of your silhouette fabric.

Use a sharp new X-acto or craft knife blade and cutting mat to carefully cut out each silhouette. Scissors will work, too, but will be more awkward. Take the time to do a nice job. Peel off the protective paper when you are finished.

Lay a silhouette on each light block, so the butterfly is centered and straight and fuse it in place. Finish these edges with a narrow matching satin stitch. A piece of lightweight tear-away stabilizer placed under the block can make this job easier. Take it slow and easy. A nice neat stitch will help you maintain that clean silhouette. Tear away the stabilizer, if used.

Now trace the smaller wings, including the dotted line, onto the non-sticky side of your iron-on interfacing. Again you will need five spiky and four smooth butterflies. Cut them roughly outside the line.

Gather together your nine wing fabrics. One at a time, lay your fabric face down on the ironing board and press smooth. You will still be able to see the printed design on the back side. Look for motifs that will make good wings. If you are using a symmetrical fabric place the interfacing (sticky side down) so the print is a mirror image on both sides. Fuse and carefully cut around the outer line of the butterfly. After the wings are cut out, cut along the dotted body lines. Now you have two perfect wings.

Center these wings on top of the corresponding silhouette block and pin them together. Sew a straight stitch around the very outer edge (1/16") of the colorful wing with matching thread. Pull all threads to the back, tie and clip.

Now finish these edges with a matching satin stitch. After each pair of wings are finished, carefully cut away the background and black silhouette fabric from behind each wing. Press flat.

Enlarge 300%

cut wings apart on
dotted line

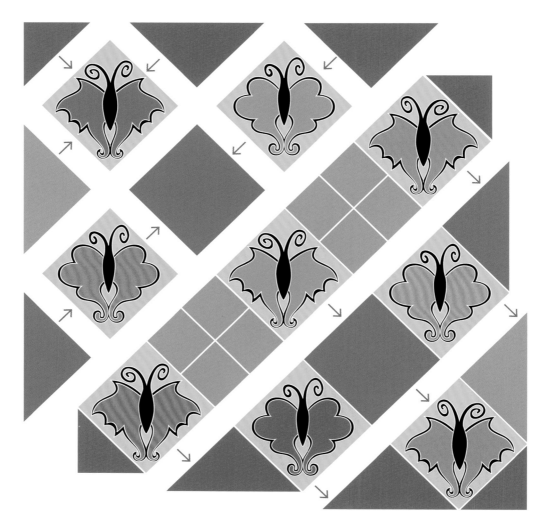

Now the body of the quilt can be assembled in diagonal rows. Press all the seams toward the dark blocks. Then starting in the top corner, stitch the rows together and press the seams open.

The border is 2½" finished, so cut five 3" selvedge to selvedge strips and piece them end to end. Cut this strip into four 51½" lengths. Cut four 3" square corner blocks.

Sew two border strips to opposite sides of the quilt and press the seams toward the border. Attach corner blocks to the ends of the remaining border strips.

Press the seams toward the border fabric. Stitch on the final borders.

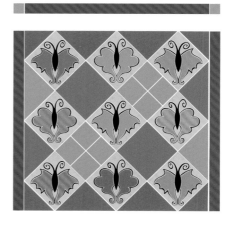

Garden Diva Butterflies

The variation quilt is exactly the same as our recipe quilt, just the fabrics have changed. But this pattern could change in so many simple ways. What if all the dark blocks were made of the same fabric. How about changing the scale to half the size? Or butterflies on a dark block instead of a light one? Remember, you get points for doing yours differently than mine!

Flower Pots in the Window

Each block of this quilt is constructed just like the Zinnia Quilt. The frames are made from two colorways of the same fabric. The dark frames contain dark pots on a light background. The light frames have light pots on a dark background.

The blocks are pieced together in a checkerboard pattern using the extra quarter inch of fabric around the frame as seam allowance.

There is also an additional border to tie it all together. The border fabrics have been carefully centered, which make lovely mitered corners for a tidy finish.

Now that your beautiful quilt top is finished, it is time to prepare it for quilting. A finished quilt is made of a sandwich of three layers that are stitched together: the top, the batting and the back. The stitching that holds them all together is called quilting.

The quilt back

As a designer, I always like to make the back of the quilt coordinate with the top. I also want the back to be interesting on its own, but I don't want the construction to take a lot of time. Basically I just want to have fun sewing the back. So my quilt backs tend to be informal; simply pieced with large cuts of fabric.

One way to coordinate the front and back of your quilt is to repeat some of the same fabrics or to use some of your leftover blocks. Another option is to pick new fabrics that share similar colors. Sometimes I like to have the two sides share a similar theme or attitude. For example, a "mysterious" quilt top, like Spiderweb Kaleidoscope, may need an equally "mysterious" back.

But other times, when I'm feeling subversive, I'll make a back that is totally unexpected. An over-the-top opulent quilt, like Oriental Carpet, might benefit from a contrasting, stark and geometric backing. The idea is that the "whole" quilt makes a statement, to which both sides contribute.

front

back

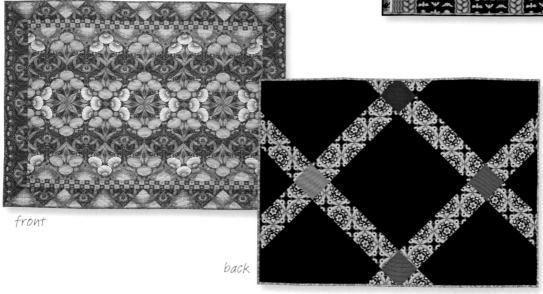

front

back

The batting

There are many high quality battings available for quilting today. I prefer a low-loft, preshrunk batting made of natural fibers or a blend of natural and synthetic fibers.

The purpose of the quilt can dictate your choice of batting. Will your quilt be used for snuggling or be hung on a wall? If your quilt will be used for warmth and comfort, you may want a thicker high-loft batting that will provide fluffiness and coziness. You will also want the batting to be machine washable. If your quilt is mainly for display, a lower loft batting would be a good choice since a lower loft batting will enable your quilt to hang flatter and be easier to maintain.

Because battings are often prepackaged in bed sizes, it is sometimes necessary to cut out the appropriate sized pieces of batting for each project although smaller pieces of batting can be pieced, butted or taped (with fusible batting tape) together.

Basting the three layers together

Before we can quilt, we need to make a secure sandwich of the three layers. This is called basting.

Construct a quilt back so it measures two inches wider than your quilt top on all sides and iron it flat. Now place it face down on a clean work table or floor that can be scratched. Using masking tape, tape the corners so the back is stretched tight. You can use the floor boards to help square up the fabric. Continue taping from opposite sides until the fabric is totally taut.

Next lay a piece of batting over the back and smooth it flat by hand. Trim the batting to be one inch smaller than the back on all sides. Place your ironed top face up over the batting. Tape the quilt top just as you did the back, beginning at the corners and stretching it tight. Continue to tape until the quilt top is square and tight.

Using curved basting safety pins, begin pinning the layers together. Start in the middle and work your way out. Work as quickly as possible. Depending on the size of your quilt, this can take an hour or several hours. Be liberal with your pins. It is better to have too many than not enough…every four inches or so. I also like to make the pins go in a variety of directions for a stronger sandwich. It is best to do your basting in a single session since your tape may loosen over time. If your quilt is large, you may actually have to sit on it to reach all the way across. In this case, lay a clean towel beneath you and lift your whole body when you move so you don't displace the layers.

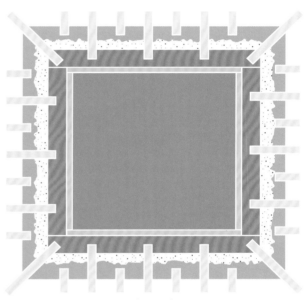

taping the quilt top

Large quilts can also be clamped (instead of taped) tight to your worktable and basted in sections. When the layers are well secured, pull off all the tape and trim the backing and the batting so it is ½" longer than the quilt top on all sides. Now you are ready to quilt.

Quilting

I am a machine quilter and when I have the time to quilt a piece myself, I use the same domestic sewing machine that I used to piece the top together. If I am pressed for time, I will send the top and back to a trusted longarm quilter. If you are sending your top to someone else to quilt, they will give you specific instructions for the size of the back and choices of batting and thread.

When I quilt, I prefer to use clean and simple quilting designs. Because the quilting is so simple, I like to use a heavier thread to make a bigger impact. I use 12 weight or topstitching thread through the needle and a matching color of regular sewing (50 weight) thread in the bobbin. Because topstitching thread is so heavy, I use a larger needle (14 or 16 topstitching) and a longer stitch.

Before you start stitching, look at your quilt top and think about the quilting possibilities. It can be helpful to photograph your quilt and print the picture so you can draw on it to test various quilting ideas. It is also good to ask yourself what colors of threads will enhance your quilt top. You can audition threads by laying them on your top to see how they look. Remember that you can change thread colors as often as you like. You aren't limited to just one color.

I usually begin quilting by either "stitching in the ditch" (up against the edge of a seam or appliqué) or echo quilting (just outside a seam or appliqué). I use my open-toed walking foot (feed dogs up) for the initial quilting, but may switch to my open-toed embroidery foot once all the major areas of the quilt top are well secured with quilting. Whenever I begin or end a row of stitching, I leave long thread tails. This is because all the threads will eventually need to be pulled to the back of the quilt, tied in a knot and buried or hidden inside the quilt.

Burying threads is easily done by pulling the top thread to the backside of your quilt and tying the top and bobbin threads together in a knot. The knot should be right up against the quilt back. Put both threads into the eye of an "easy-threading" or "self-threading" hand needle and poke the needle back into the same hole where the threads came out. Bring the needle up again in a different spot and give the threads a tug. You will hear the knot popping inside the quilt. Cut off the excess thread.

Feed Dogs Up or Down?

If you are using a domestic sewing machine for your quilting, there are two techniques that you can use... with the feed dogs up or down. Feed dogs are the little teeth beneath the presser foot that grip and pull the fabric through the machine. But you can also drop those teeth so they don't touch the fabric at all. When the teeth are dropped, you will also switch to your darning or free-motion quilting foot which just hovers over the surface of the quilt. Then you will be able to guide and glide the quilt in any direction that you would like. Free motion quilting gives you the freedom to "draw" with thread.

Very straight lines and soft curves are easier to sew with the feed dogs up. Flowing, wavy, organic shapes are easier to make with the feed dogs down. Both of these techniques are valid and will add to the final detail, texture and rhythm of your quilt. They can both be used in the same project, as well, and both take some practice to perfect. There are many good classes and books to help you learn more about quilting techniques, but the best training comes with doing.

Quilting Options

There are several options for quilting your quilts today. You can quilt them by hand, with a domestic sewing machine or on a longarm system.

Longarm quilting machines are larger than domestic sewing machines and they can either be stationary (sitting on a table) or mobile (placed on a gliding platform). On a stationary longarm, the quilt is guided under the needle by hand. The mobile longarm quilting machines are guided by the operator over a stationary quilt.

Easy Threading Needles

Easy threading needles are one of my essential quilting tools. They have made my sewing life so much easier that I cannot live without them at this point. Instead of the tedious job of poking your threads through the tiny eye of a regular needle, an easy threading needle has an opening at the top which connects to the eye. This allows you to snap the thread into the eye very quickly. The quality of these needles vary. A poorly made needle can tear your threads and make your life miserable so invest in the most reliable brands of needles and test each needle in the pack. A good easy threading needle is worth its weight in gold!

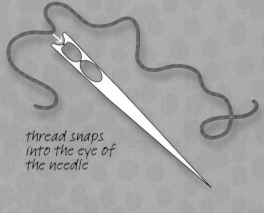

thread snaps into the eye of the needle

Binding Your Quilt

After you have finished quilting, press your quilt flat and trim off the excess batting and backing so they are flush with the front, the corners are square and the sides perpendicular.

Then it is time to finish the edges of your quilt. This is called binding. Binding creates the fine final frame around your quilt. It is also part of the overall composition of the quilt, so it is worthwhile to consider it seriously.

Bindings can be subtle or bold, matching or contrasting, one color or many colors. I always audition several options to find the most effective solution.

To bind your quilt you will need four 1½" strips that are ½" longer than the sides of your quilt. First take one binding strip and fold the ends over ¼" so the wrong sides are together. Lay this strip face down on top of the quilt and pin it to the corresponding edge. Stitch ¼" from the edge, backstitching at both ends. Pull the threads to the front.

Press the strip in place to set the seam. Then fold the binding back and press it so it goes beyond the edge. Flip the quilt over and fold and press the cut edge of the binding strip so it meets the raw edge of the quilt. Fold the strip again to the back of the quilt and pin it in place covering the stitching line.

At this point you can either hand stitch or machine stitch the binding in place. If your quilt is for use, machine stitching will make it stronger. If your quilt is for display, hand sewing will make it look nicer.

To machine stitch, sew on the front side of the quilt right in the ditch next to the edge of the binding. You will only be able to sew a few inches at a time as you will have to remove the pins that are underneath your quilt as you reach them.

To hand sew the binding, simply use a matching thread and slip stitch it to the quilt's back. Repeat this process for the opposite edge of the quilt. Then again for the remaining two sides.

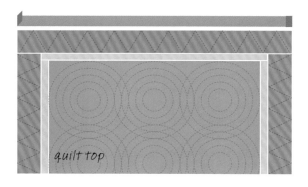

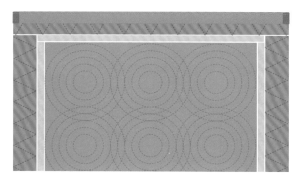

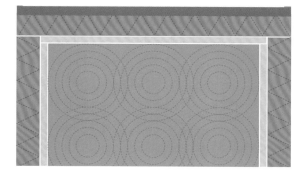

Wrap Up

After studying these energetic quilts and discovering how easy they are to make, you should be looking at those big beautiful fabrics with new appreciation. Not only are they exciting right off the bolt, but they can contribute to some wonderful patchwork quilts.

By learning to recognize the character in the cloth and knowing the basics of patchwork, you can focus on the fabric's potential right away. So pull those "personality prints" out of hibernation and let them guide your next creative patchwork project.

Acknowledgements

Thanks to Linda Teufel, editor and founder of Dragon Threads, for embracing this project and holding my hand through it all. And many thanks to Kim Koloski for making every page of this book sing!

I also want to acknowledge my friends Susan Tempin, Melissa Peda and Juanita Whiting for all their enthusiasm and help making so many fabric projects materialize.

And, as always, thanks to my husband, Greg Gantner, for his stunning photography and his endless patience for putting up with an obsessed quilter year after year.

All quilts were designed by Jane Sassaman and many talented people have helped with piecing and quilting.

All fabrics used are designed by Jane Sassaman for FreeSpirit Fabrics, www.freespiritfabric.com

To find a list of vendors for Jane's fabrics visit
www.janesassaman.com

Visit Janes Idea Book for updates,
www.sassaman.blogspot.com

Wild Tulip Wallpaper designed by William Morris is courtesy of William Morris Designs and Patterns by Norah Gillow, 1988, published by Crescent Books, Distributed by Crown Publishers, Inc. New York, New York.

Rulers, templates, mats, rotary cutters courtesy of Omnigrid, Prym Consumer USA, Spartanburg, SC 29304, www.dritz.com/brands/omnigrid

Fast 2 Cut-Fussy Cutter 3" and 6.5" Diamond Ruler Set by Jan Krentz www.jankrentz.com

Bernina sewing machine courtesy of Bernina
3702 Prairie Lake Court,
Aurora, IL 60504
www.berninausa.com

I'm proud to be a Bernina Artisan

BERNINA✚

Sewing support:

Quilts pieced by Juanita Whiting, Woodstock, IL:
Bleeding Heart Star
Lacy Star
Garden Diva Butterflies

Quilts pieced and quilted by Audrey Esarey, Louisville, KY:
Emerald Jack Star

Quilts pieced by Jean Leeson, Madison, WI
www.JeanLeeson.com
Gothic Window
Spiderweb Kaleidoscope
Solar Star
Cosmic Star

Quilts quilted by Jean Leeson, Madison, WI
www.JeanLeeson.com
Solar Star

Quilts quilted by Risë Levine, Risë's Pieces Custom Longarm Quilting, Springfield, MO:
Barn Dance
Primrose Variations
Bouquet Reflections

Quilts quilted by Sandra Sims, Heirloom Originals, Petersburg, VA:
Jack's Journey

Quilts quilted by Janice Head, Head to Sew Quilts, Windsor, CA, www.headtosew.com:
Sweet Potato Vines and Rose Hips
Circus Bars
Butterfly Bars
Picnic Quilt
Lacy Star

Quilts quilted by Marilyn Karper, Karper Quilting Service, Overland Park, KS, www.karperquilting.com:
Paradise Garden
Early Bird Hearts

Quilts quilted by Jean Shute, Otis Orchard, WA:
Turquoise Four Patch
Dragonfly Moon
Hothouse Kaleidoscope
Oriental Carpet
Midnight Coneflowers
Gothic Windows
Peacock Reflections
Glowing Crosses
Rowdy Barn Raising
Magic Forest Kaleidoscope
Gypsy Scarf
Spider Web Kaleidoscope
Cosmic Star
Mexican Hearts

Quilts quilted by Pam McIntyre, Quilting Makes the Quilt, Gainesville, FL
www.quiltingmakesthequilt.com
Hugs and Kisses

Quilted By Kathy Balmert, Quilty Pleasures, Dublin, OH, www.quilty-pleasures.com
Morning Song
Summer Serenade
Primrose Wreath
Bleeding Heart Star